How to be a Grandfather

"There are many points at which one forgets one is reading a translation at all... This is great poetry of childhood – but simultaneously, and not coincidentally, it is among the finest poetry of old age.

"Hearing Eye deserve our gratitude for their publication of How to be a Grandfather, which I strongly recommend for the accomplishment of the translator and the thought-provoking quality of much of what is translated." – Glyn Pursglove – *Acumen*

to Martin
with all best wishes

Victor Hugo

How to be a Grandfather

(L'Art d'être Grand-Père)

translated and introduced by

Timothy Adès

Tim

The Complete Edition,
with other poems

Hearing Eye

Published by Hearing Eye 2012

Hearing Eye, Box 1, 99 Torriano Avenue
London NW5 2RX, UK
email: hearing_eye@torriano.org
www.hearingeye.org

—∾—

ISBN: 978-1-905082-66-7

Reprinted Translations:
'Moscow, Waterloo, St Helena' appeared in *Comparative Criticism* and in the *Journal of the Napoleonic Society of America.*
'As Boaz Was Dozing' appeared in *Modern Poetry in Translation.*
'Advice to Lovers' appeared in *Acumen.*

The translation of the sonnet by Jean Cassou appeared in *Comparative Criticism* (Cambridge U.P.) and in *33 Sonnets of the Resistance* (Arc Publications). It is reprinted here by kind permission of Éditions Gallimard, as is 'The Legacy' (Le Legs) by Robert Desnos, from *Destinée Arbitraire* (Éditions Gallimard, 1975). Thanks are due to the editors of all these publications.

—∾—

Hearing Eye is represented by
Inpress Ltd in the UK – see www.inpressbooks.co.uk
Trade distribution: Central Books, 99 Wallis Road, London E9 5LN

Cover photo: Victor, Georges and Jeanne in 1881 (detail)
by Carl Lundelius (Roger-Viollet/Top Foto)

Designed by Martin Parker at www.silbercow.co.uk
Printed by Catford Print Centre, London

About Victor Hugo

Victor Hugo is best known to English-speakers by the screen and musical versions of just two of his novels, *Les Misérables* and *Notre-Dame de Paris*. Yet he created a torrent of wonderful poetry, plays, novels and political speeches. He is France's greatest poet and perhaps greatest writer, commemorated by a big street or square in hundreds of towns and villages. More than that, he was a great human being, he was and still is a worldwide symbol of liberty. Twice a Deputy and twice a Senator, he never stood for President of France, but two million people went to his funeral.

Why then do we English-speakers not know him? In middle and later life Hugo was fiercely hostile to the idea of monarchy as he knew it, and to the church (though he always believed in God). Some of us may sympathise, but many do not hold, or care for, such strong views. Hugo increasingly deplored his country's old autocratic kings; he despised Napoleon III, an elected President who had made himself Emperor and had banished Hugo for resisting. Hugo stayed in exile in the Channel Islands for two decades until this emperor fell. The British experience of monarchy has been quite different from the French. France never had real constitutional monarchy, Britain never developed republican institutions. What the British understand by 'kings' and 'princes' is not what Hugo understood, at all.

Again, Hugo, like most French intellectuals since Voltaire's time, was strongly opposed to the church. He stood for tolerance; he was against the church as a dominant force. He disliked organised religion in general, a view not always well received in Britain, and fairly unpopular in the United States. The real point was that he disliked any kind of authority.

Nearly all Hugo's books, whether prose or poetry, were extremely successful. *L'Art d'être Grand-Père* was no exception. Hugo's French public, reading him avidly, knew and still knows what to expect of him. The French know his opinions; but many who come to him now in English translation, whatever their background and their beliefs, may not know his cast of mind, and may be taken aback by his vehemence. Enough to say that he had his reasons. For one thing, the Archbishop of Paris had crowned the usurper.

Childhood fascinated Hugo. For him, children are innocents from paradise, they rejuvenate the old; perhaps they even amaze, delight and console the wild beasts in the zoo. He cannot see in young children any trace of Original Sin: far from it, if little innocents grow into flawed adolescents, like the lad who threw a stone at Jeanne, he forgives the culprit and the culprit's mother, blaming instead the priest – and forgiving him too. He is a happy grandfather who gladly accepts the demands and manipulative tactics of the young. He knows they are using him. He knows they are the future, they must one day take charge. All is forgiven as their insouciant fun and laughter transform his declining years.

Introducing this Complete Edition

It takes some time to grasp the enormous, overpowering scale of Victor Hugo. I brought out a shorter version of this book in 2002, published, like the present edition, by Hearing Eye. Translating with rhyme, if done well, is a very demanding labour of love: I had done as much as I could: I left much of *L'Art d'être Grand-Père* completely unexplored, likewise Hugo's tumultuous life story, which is summarised for the reader in this volume. From that intermediate point I have now finished the task of presenting this, the great man's last volume of poems. New treasures have been unearthed, a bigger and deeper picture revealed.

What has been added in this complete edition? There is more magnificent rhetoric, and much more about the wild animals at the zoo. Hugo ponders the animal kingdom and the questions raised by Darwin, but as a poet, not as a scientist: he asserts the innocence of childhood and the rightness of the affections in man and nature, against received doctrine, as he sees it. He upholds freedom against authority, humanity against oppression. In the long final poem, beyond any limits of religion, he looks for God and ultimate truth.

This completed book is a typically Hugolian monster, larger than life, a work of huge energy and generosity. Judged by normal standards, it may be too big by half. For all its many delights and wonders, it may please neither those who want an easy read for family and friends, nor those arid critics who disapprove of children, grandfathers, animals, and rhymes. Never mind! Please accept Victor Hugo as you find him, as he really is. – T.A.

CONTENTS

I On Guernsey

i. The Contented Exile

O Solitude! Silence! The call of the wild!
The soul is at peace there, austerely beguiled,
In shadows unknown that we seem to have lightened.
I go to the forests in hopes to be frightened;
From the branches' unwelcoming throng I procure
An enjoyment, a thrill that is somehow obscure,
And I find an oblivion close to the tomb.
But I'm not to be quenched; we can flare in the gloom,
Stand alone in the undercroft under high heaven,
And quake in the wind of the great empyrean.
It is no diminution in man to have thrown,
Down the dark well of duty, a questioning stone.
From high up we see right, from far off we see clear;
And our mind is aware it can burnish its power,
Can advance in its consciousness, as it ascends,
And can grow and shine brighter where worldliness ends.
So I go to the wild without leaving the world.

Though a dreamer may come to the depths of the weald,
Or the crests of the cliffs, to have peace, and to ponder
The hugeness of dusk, he is not cut asunder
From earth, and from men. I've seen many of these;
Don't you feel that I need to withdraw to the trees?
Don't you feel that deep yearnings for truth and for peace,
And for justice, for reason and light, must arise
In the depths of the soul, after so many lies?

All men are my brothers, well-loved, far away:
I am with them; their story, I watch and I weigh.

With compassion I soften each soul that's rough-hewn;
Leaning over the peoples, I pour from my urn;
I pour it, and fill it, in endless cascade,
But the great wordless woods are my shelter and shade.

I've seen so close the huddled crowds,
Shouts, shocks and good grey heads besmirched;
Riots raise up so many cowards,
Judges who better had been judged;
Priests by whom God is served and soiled,
Whose preaching fails with proof reversed;
I've seen the blight our beauty heralds,
Falsehood in truth, in good the worst;
Vaunting at triumph's arch, the void.
I've seen what bites, and bends, and crawls;
I am defeated, weakened, old:
My joy, to dream in calm of shade;
I muse, and bleed; and if a god
Bade me return to crowded halls,
And fame, love, youth, strength, victory,
I'm glad of my wildwood's hides and holes,
Not being too sure that I'd agree.

ii. What Is This Earth?

What is this earth? A storm of souls.
Benighted on uncharted seas,
We miss the port and hit the shoals;
Gales of desires and agonies,
Dark loves and sorrows, vows and cries!
Ambition, fortune, and success
Plant a loose woman's short-lived kiss.
What do I know? says Job, and sighs;
What do I think? Pascal replies.
Some evil well of monstrous things
Spews popes and emperors and kings;
Fate spins the capstan till it brings
The same floods and catastrophes
That shook our new philosophies;
In gnashing void and perjured chaos
Man in the end can clearly see,
Above our funerals, falls and failures,
That Innocence has sovereignty.
Given the human heart and spirit,
Night of the past, night yet to inherit,
All hatreds, conflicts, wars and pains,
Our progress stopped by dragging chains;
Even the best not spared remorse;
The winds from deep in weeping skies
That blast us daily from our course:-
Beneath such black and tangled boughs
It does us good to recognize,
Beyond the teeming woes that rise,
Like veils, between us and the skies,
A peace, profound, all made of stars.
That's why God lets the poets creep
About the cradles lapped in sleep.

iii. Jean Makes Her Entry

Jean talks: she burbles, sweet and low;
Tells nature things she doesn't know,
Tells groaning waves and moaning woods,
Flowers and nests, all heaven, the clouds,
Offering insights, by a smile,
From shimmering dream and roving soul:
A formless murmur, blurred and hazed.
Old grandpa God gives ear, amazed.

iv. Victor Vanquished

Our time is one of frenzies and of wars.
I am a warrior; I've fought emperors,
Fought the vile throng of Sodoms, heard again
The mass of waters and the mass of men
Roaring against me, and I would not yield.
Waves crashed against me on the battlefield,
The shadow's and the storm's full force assailed,
And all the great Gehenna surged and railed.
Rock-like, I never bent my head, for I
Cannot be frightened by a funeral sky:
Others may tremble on the dark cave's rim,
I do not fear to plunge in hellish stream.
When tyrants hurled at us, from clouds sublime,
Their sable thunderbolts that flashed with crime,
I have thrown sombre verses at the sinister
Transients, dragging down each king and minister,
False gods, false precepts, sceptres towering high,
Thrones linked to scaffolds, swords of infamy:
I've dragged them helter-skelter down to hell.
I've faced the giants of brute force, that swell
And rear erect on heaped-up nothingness:

Caesars and autocrats and princes, yes,
All those whom mortals worship, loathe, adore:
I've faced the Jupiters of total power
For forty years, victorious, running wild!
Look now: I'm vanquished by a little child.

v. *The Other One*

Come, George. The sons of our sons are enchanting!
They are young voices that sing at the dawning,
Light in our joyless homes, the returning
Of roses and springtime, of life and morning!
Their laugh makes our eyelids wet with tears
And sets the old stones of our threshold shaking;
Their radiant faces dispel the fears
Of heavy old age and the cold grave yawning.
They take us back to our earliest years,
To be soft and simple and glad without reason,
An airy vagueness the blithe heart taking:
We see ourselves in our flowering season:
Grandfathers return to the day's awaking.
The jubilant young join the happy old man,
Little children who let us be little again.
Serenely we witness, among all these
Bright souls, our dark soul take to the trees.

vi. George And Jean

A child makes me a stupid ass:
In George and Jean I have a brace.
One is my guide and one my star.
I run to where their voices are;
Jean is ten months and George is two,
Divinely gauche in all they do;
And when they try to speak, we seem
To sense a passing, holy dream.
I who am evening, I the night,
Pale, cold, and doomed to fade from sight,
Call them, with love, the dawning light.
Their riddling speech expands my brain,
As they confer, concur, explain.
My thoughts are disarranged, dispersed:
My hopes, my plans, the best, the worst,
Collapse in their relaxing glow,
And I'm a star-struck so-and-so.
Sin's lure, and our appointed lot,
May jolt and jar, but touch me not.
The tottering child's our safest prop.
I watch, and listen, and I stop
Worrying: I am good, and nice,
Take innocence's pure advice.
I've always done so; I've not known,
Whether elated or cast down,
Sweetness to match our blissful dream
At a pure being's humble flame:
Thus, in our black and tarnished times,
From nests and cradles, daylight climbs.

I watch them sleep. Their brows are calm,
Part shaded by a tiny palm,

Part brighter than a rising star.
I wonder what their visions are:
George dreams of cakes, of wondrous toys,
The dog, cat, cockerel; Jean enjoys
Her angels. Then they waken, smiling.

They reach us just as we are failing.

They babble: they are chattering,
As woodland flower to limpid spring,
As Charles their father used to do
With their Aunt Adela, long ago;
As I with you in sunny Rome,
Dear brothers! at our father's home,
The barracks: as he watched, we rode,
Playing at gee-gees, on his sword.

Jean's eyes, forget-me-nots of sight!
Frail fingers, splayed to hold the night!
Her arms, two wings for angel-flight!
Songs, almost wordless, recondite,
For handsome George, the favoured mite.
No language this, but infinite
Reason, as innocent and noble
As winds' and waves' and forests' burble.
Jason and Palinurus heard
The siren softly speak this word,
Dark music by deep water blurred;
May-music, such that, strangely moved,
We say 'I love', or 'Once I loved':
The vague translucent speech that spills
From infants at Life's window-sills,
Who baulk at April, at a loss,
And hum and buzz at Spring's great glass.
These mystic words of George and Jean!
Poems of the robin and the swan,

Queries of bumble-bees, a silly
Quiz to wise sparrows from the lily;
The bass-note of God's harmony,
Vast, whispering, awesome sanctity,
Murmuring, stammering reverie,
Which may enlighten you and me:
For little ones, a day ago,
Were still in heaven, and they know
Much more than we do, here below.
Jean! George! I love those chirps of yours,
Uncertain as the songs of stars!
We're lightened, brightened by their glance:
Loved strangers, what's your provenance?
Jean gapes, and George has fearless eyes:
They lurch, still drunk on paradise.

vii. Sometimes, I'm Full of Horror

Sometimes, I'm full of horror for this earth:
My verses seem a crater's open mouth;
    I'm fiercely moved, as though
I'm a great tree caught in a monstrous storm;
My heart flames, and my granite flanks deform
    To lava's liquid flow.

Is nothing true? The pen's backed by the fist;
The robes of judge and virgin, wife and priest,
    Tell lies – they're lying now.
Dogma drinks blood, the altar blesses crime;
The verities, unsmiling and sublime,
    Blush crimson at their brow.

Sinister light of kings is on our heads;
Temples are hellish; by our lurid feasts
    Blue heaven is obscured;
The soul goes listing like a ship of doom;
And all religions, groping in the gloom,
    Take demons for the Lord!

O! Who shall arm me with tremendous words?
O! I shall tear these bibles and accords,
    These holy books and laws:
With mighty voice I'll cry catastrophe,
Seize in my screed you sons of sophistry,
    You tyrants in my claws.

So, pale with furious rage, I shake and seethe:
Who knows what swarms of black-winged eagles wreathe
    Their whirlwinds in my skies?
Death! War! Inside of me, a hell-hag grows:
Everywhere, evil! Then I see a rose –
    Which promptly pacifies.

viii. The Joy of Things: Lætitia rerum

Everywhere, a sudden ferment.
Winter hurries off, disrobes;
Old year drops her faded garment,
Earth puts on her finest robes.

All is new, proud, debonair.
Round us, youth's awakenings;
Devil-beauty everywhere
Sparkles, preens in limpid springs.

Trees start flirting. Flowers choose
Which of them is loveliest:
All display their gaudy hues,
Even the very homeliest.

Tufts are spurting from the rock;
Light leaves by the air are kissed.
June adores these tiny folk
Of the heath, in Sunday best.

It's a proper festival;
Coarse-grained thistle's mood is festal.
In the summer's banquet-hall
Stars light up the tiers of crystal.

Now, it's hay-time: next, the grain.
In the copse, the reaper sleeps.
Scented breezes all retain
Perfume of the grass he reaps.

Nightingale is singing there;
All the chrysalids have gone.
Earthworm climbs to take the air,
Flings to the nettles his old gown.

Water-boatmen tour the pond;
Blue skies frame the trellis-shade;
Breezes stir the reedy frond;
Tiny insects serenade.

Wasp and hungry bee take wing,
Hornet's at his look-out post.
Wayside pub is opening;
Quaff the perfumes: spring's mine host!

Bumble-bee who loves excess
Smoothes his shirt, adjusts his tie:
Bud of the pink's his brimming glass;
Lily, his white napery.

Crimson draughts, and gold, the fly
Sips from flowers that shyly close;
Bar-fly is the butterfly,
Toper's tavern is the rose.

Ecstasy and joy imbibed!
Drunkenness is deliverance!
Not one flower is inscribed
'Solemn League of Temperance'.

Nature in her pomp and bloom
Gushes, bursts a thousand-fold:
Heaven is a priceless tome
That the dawn has edged with gold.

My children, in your shining eyes
To me the empyrean appears;
The spring lives in your gaieties,
And the dawn rises in your tears.

ix. Two Little Hands in Mine

Two little hands in mine, we'll go;
I love the woods, where the white roe
Leads dappled bucks; where deer with fawns
Halt, startled by the shady fronds:
Such nervous creatures, taking fright
At a leaf's twitch, however slight.
Trees have a deepness which imparts
That only Eden, where true hearts
Entwine, is real. Love, and the nest!
There's nothing good in all the rest.
Theocritus in sacred grove
Heard the wild dancing-women move:
And I shall stroll with George and Jean,
Hear him advise and her explain,
Dear loves, in turn. A patriarch
Leading the young, I'll slow my walk
To keep beside their little stride,
And match their meals, their games and hours:
They shall eat blackberries, and pick flowers.
Great forest-murmur, solace-giving!
April with calm and balm comes roving;
I have no business here but loving.

x. Spring

All's radiant, loving, sweet and bright.
The birds carouse in air and light;
The soul sees in the infinite,
Or seems to see, a great big smile.
You kings! Why banish? Why exile?
Do you ban summer? Exile flowers?
Can you prevent the warm bright airs
From being boundless, endless, free,
Balm of my banned obscurity?
Can you curtail the surging main,
The bounding foam? Can you contain
The Spring, who spreads his perfumes wide,
A spendthrift, on the crazy side,
Or the vast Sun? You have no way
To keep from me a single ray.
No. I forgive you. Carry on!
Survive, reign longer, if you can!
You may seize empires; I shall pluck, all
The while, a sprig of honeysuckle,
And carry off my conquered flower;
And if above me in the bower
A loud male bird molests his mate,
Is it my business? No – and yet
I intervene, and tell them: Peace,
Birds in the forest, if you please!
With my big voice I reconcile:
A shock can make sour lovers smile...
No river, stream, or rock for me;
A narrow lawn, beside the sea,
A little pond: no bitterness.
I like this humble nook. There's space,
High overhead, where eagles pass,
Stars shine, and mighty Boreas

Wanders about, distractedly.
This modest ground and arching sky
Are mine: the blooms and greenery
Love me; I find, increasingly,
I'm proud to lose my memory.
Here in my woods, what chance at all,
How should I manage to recall
That someone walks the earth afar,
Banishing, reigning, waging war?
Alone with the immensity,
Deep sky of summer over me,
Winds murmuring like a lyre, or softer,
I hear, in the garden, children's laughter.

xi. Open Windows

Morning – asleep

Voices. Light on my eyelid. In full cry,
Bell of St Peter's. Bathers' merry shouts:
This way! No, that way! Nearer! Further back!
Birds twitter: Jean does too. George calls to her.
Cocks crow, a trowel scrapes a roof; horses
Pass in the lane; a rasping scythe cuts grass.
Impacts, impressions. Roofers overhead.
The harbour's noises. Hiss of hot machines.
The gusting of a military band.
A hubbub on the quay. French voices. Thanks.
Morning. Goodbye. It must be late, because
My robin redbreast's come up close, to sing.
The roar of distant hammers at a forge.
Clacking of water. Steamship's puffing breath.
A fly comes in. Vast wheezing of the sea.

xii. An Absence

O why did he leave us, the dear little love?
They're a light in our darkness, turned suddenly off.
We think that these children are ours, but they prove
To be somebody else's. – 'Well, that's as may be;
But you still have a couple, old boy, don't you see?' -
Yes, I do. They are two, and they could have been three.
Look, it's time for a walk in the shade of the glen,
Where the number of birds to God only is known,
And they fly away too, and are vanished and gone.

He has his white hat on, she's flaunting her toes.
Side by side to adventure my family goes,
All heaven is bright and I'm pushing the pram.
Like the garden of Eden, the plain is in bloom;
Beneath the old willows a lizard is running,
And there, in the fronds, robin redbreast is singing.
Jean's fifteen months old, George is double that figure,
Protective, a regular man, so much bigger!
He loves all the girls with their pretty pink fingers,
Shows off his big hands, for he soon will be three,
Compares as he comments, ingeniously,
Shows Jean to the villagers, laughs as he strides.
Jean laughs at his laughter, she toddles, she rides,
She's a queen on a throne, she is beautiful too,
And the oak tells the chestnut, the elm bowing low
Points her out to the maple: all things in the wildwood,
All under high heaven, pay homage to childhood.

I'm a big boy, thinks George, in the midst of his laughter:
Jean trusts my good sense: I've a child to look after.
Yes, fiercely protective is what he's become
Of this mite intermittently sucking her thumb.

Now the paths are all tangled, we're losing our way,
And in all the wood's shadows the butterflies play.
George is eager to run; Jean is happy and gay;
In their presence I falter, I stammer and sway.
What adorable joy! What a couple of charmers!
How splendid the anthem hid deep in their murmurs!
Jean claims every bird, on the bough or the wing;
George's old jumping jack has a rickety spring,
So he thoughtfully guts it; their chatter and cries
Seem to rouse in the shadows a staring of eyes.
Eating apples and medlars, George brings me his toy;
I know more about Man and his ways than the boy,
And the secrets of Fate, so I soon get the jack
To start jumping again, with a wire in his back.
Look, don't walk in the grass, George: it's terribly wet.
As the wind rocks the tree-tops, Jean rocks her Babette.
The presence of God can be felt in this wood
That blends its sweet calm with the rapturous mood
Of brother and sister. One person's in charge:
Both Jean and myself take our orders from George;
And Nanny is singing those Norman refrains
Which, as twilight is falling, you hear in the lanes.
She sets George's foot tapping and Jean's two hands clapping;
I beam and I bask in this marvellous 'earful',
But under the laughter you sense I am tearful:
Old trees! you can tell, and you always have known,
That I'll never forget him, the little one gone.

II Jean Asleep – I

The Siesta

The day half-gone, she takes her little nap.
She must dream more than one who is grown up:
Earth starves the eye that feasted on the ethereal.
She turns again to Cherubino, Ariel,
Puck and Titania and their fairy bands,
And while she lies asleep, God warms her hands.
What would we only give to witness, deep
Down in that hallowed and refulgent sleep,
Unfolding in the gloom to our surprise,
Those dazzling visions, each a paradise,
And stars that come and tell her to be good:
How rare a sight to witness, if we could!
Now, at midday, the fiery sun's effect
Is calming; nature stops to recollect,
Stands still to listen; for an interval
Of time, the leaf that trembles most of all
Forgets to shake; the nests all stop their cheeping.
It's now Jean has her lovely way of sleeping.
Her mother breathes again in brief repose;
You can be wearied, waiting on a rose.
The wee bare feet, that totter as they tread,
Sleep, and the cradle's like a haloed head,
Celestial, ringed with formless azure haze:
You'd say, a cloud that's fashioned out of lace.
In that cool crib you see her as a glow
Of pink, deep down inside a furbelow.
We look at her, we laugh, all happiness:
She is a shining star, with littleness.
The shade adores her, lets its feelings show;
The wind restrains its breath, too shy to blow;

She in her mother's alcove plain and pure
Opens an eye from which the sunbeams pour,
Stretches an arm and waves each foot in turn;
And watching faces in the empyrean
Lean down to listen to her heavenly murmur.
With tender voice, eyes widening to cover
The child that God makes radiant, her mother
Looks for the sweetest name she can confer
On her joy, her angel-flower, her chimera;
And then she speaks. "Awake again, you horror!"

III The Moon

i. Jean was Sitting on the Grass

Jean was sitting on the grass,
Pink and thoughtful. Up I came.
"Tell me, Jean,
Is there anything you want?"
I obey these little loves,
Watch, and try to understand
All that passes (bless them) through their heads.
Jean replied: "I'd like to see
Some animals." I pointed out
("Look!") an ant, in the grass.
Jean was only half contented. "No,
Animals are big," she said.

Bigness is their dream. The sea
Draws them to its edges, dandles them
With its throaty singing, fascinates
With its shadows and the wind's
Scary flight;
They love terror, need the marvellous.
"Look, I have no elephant:
Would you fancy something else?
You deserve it, Jean," I said.
"Speak." Her tiny finger swivelled up
To the sky. "*That.*" Evening had begun.
There on the horizon I could see,
Rising, the enormous moon.

ii. Evening

The fog is cold and the heather is grey;
The cattle-herds go to the drinking-troughs;
The moon breaks out from behind black clouds,
A brightness coming as if by surprise.

I don't know where and I don't know when,
Old Yannick was blowing his chanter and drone.

The traveller walks and the moor is brown;
A shadow behind and a shadow before;
There's white in the west and light in the east;
Here dusk, and there the light of the moon.

I don't know where and I don't know when,
Old Yannick was blowing his chanter and drone.

The sorceress sits and her lip goes long;
The spider fixes her web to the tile;
The will-o'-the-wisp has a goblin glow
Like a pistil of gold in a tulip's bowl.

I don't know where and I don't know when,
Old Yannick was blowing his chanter and drone.

There are ketches and coasters out on the sea;
There's shipwreck in wait for the shuddering mast;
The wind says: to-morrow! the water says: now!
There are voices heard and they speak despair.

I don't know where and I don't know when,
Old Yannick was blowing his chanter and drone.

The coach from Avranches to Fougères
Has a crack of the whip like a lightning-flash;

There's many a noise grows loud from the dark,
And they mingle together, to float on the air.

I don't know where and I don't know when,
Old Yannick was blowing his chanter and drone.

In the depths of the forest, bright torches shine;
A graveyard clings to a mountain-top;
Where does God find all the blackness he pours
Into nights that fall, into hearts that break?

I don't know where and I don't know when,
Old Yannick was blowing his chanter and drone.

There are puddles of silver that shake on the sands;
The osprey is close to the cliffs of chalk;
The shepherd is watching across the wind
The devils in vague and monstrous flight.

I don't know where and I don't know when,
Old Yannick was blowing his chanter and drone.

There are plumes of grey from the chimney-stacks;
The wood-cutter passes, bearing his load;
The noise of a stream in spate is heard,
With the crashing of branches, dragged along.

I don't know where and I don't know when,
Old Yannick was blowing his chanter and drone.

The great fierce wolves have a starving dream;
The river is racing, the cloud takes flight;
Behind the panes where the lamp is bright
Are the glowing cheeks of the very young.

I don't know where and I don't know when,
Old Yannick was blowing his chanter and drone.

iii. Ah! So You Want the Moon?

Ah! So you want the moon? Where? Down there in that well?
No, in the sky. All right, let's have a go!... *I can't.*
It happens every time. My darlings, you decide
You want to have the moon, and so I launch my hands,
And try to catch the orb of Phoebe in her flight.
The dear sweet stroke of luck of being Grand-papa
Has fallen on my head and left me slightly cracked.
I look at you and feel Fate may have shut me off
From happiness, but can't entirely strike me down.
Let's have a chat, though. George, d'you see it? Jean, do you?
God knows us, and he knows what grand-papas may do,
Because He is Himself a sort of grand-papa.
God has to be on guard against us every day;
His fear is the old man who wants to please a child.
He knows your word is my command and I'll obey;
He wants us not to touch the stars and that is why
He hangs them on the highest nails at the top of the sky.

iv. Oh! How Greedy They Are!

Oh! How greedy they are! is their mother's refrain;
They have to be given again and again
Orchard-apples, wild cherries, the cakes from the table,
And if they hear cows giving voice in the stable,
Quick! Milk! and in sight of a packet of candy
Their cries come as thick as the forest of Bondy.
Just hark at them now – they're demanding the moon!

Well, why not? Your colossus collapses quite soon,
But the small are amazingly, dazzlingly grand.
It's true that their appetites tend to expand,
And I'm thoughtful about the acquisitive soul
Sees all Space in the shadows and asks for it whole.
So: why not the moon? You may answer: what of it?
Well! If it were mine, they'd be welcome to have it.

Yes, without really knowing the gain or the risk,
I'd present them, dear moon, with your shadowy disc,
Your sky, from which Swedenborg never broke free,
Your mysterious, fathomless riddle-me-ree!
Yes, I'd make them a present (I'd tell them: Take care)
Of your mask, darkly watching the clouds of the air,
Your craters all twisted and gouged by black gales,
Your solitudes dark and forgotten, your vales
Whether smiling or horrible, Edens or hells,
And the vision and view of your colourless hills.
Yes, I think, after all, that these reverent elves
Could make much better use of the moon than ourselves:
They would give it their yearning, their hope and their prayer,
They would let the adventuress shepherd and steer
Their little hearts' thoughts to the great God above.
For they sleep in the night with their dreams on the move:

Children's dreams outrun ours, flying further and higher:
As did once the apostles, now children inspire
All my faith: little loves without rancour and fear,
I would grant what they want in the heavenly sphere,
If it only were mine. If a girl wants a planet,
The one of her choice should be hers: she should own it.
And can't we do better than stand on our rights?
Wouldn't kings be astonished that dear little mites
Could lay claim to a world! I would watch them with pleasure.
Yes, that's what I'd offer to each little treasure:
To you monarchs of love I would give, if I might,
Those galaxies bathed in mysterious light,
That are steered by the sprites of the shadows who minister,
Shadows and planets, vast, rounded and sinister.
Why? I can see you: you never have erred,
And therefore I trust you. It's often occurred,
When I ponder how great is the innocent heart,
And my thoughts to the infinite limits depart,
That, gripped by ecstatic and numinous wonder,
I sense in the distant unknowable Yonder
A god who's undreamed-of, and higher than ours,
By whose bounty our souls can be given the stars.

IV Poem of the Zoo

(Poème du Jardin des Plantes)

i. Buffon, That Splendid Man

Buffon, that splendid man, created
This public garden, imitated
From the old Roman paradise,
And stocked it full of bears more wise
Than many a disputatious don
Who stands erect at the Sorbonne;
All so that Jean can go, with Alice.
He thought a lightly tigered Paris,
Graced with this social variant,
The animal, might well enchant
The smiling soul of Jean, whom he
Foresaw. I hail him, gratefully.
The deeper insight of the child
Yearns, now and then, to see the wild;
Paternal Buffon, paying off
The words that flowed beneath his cuff,
Made for our angel-envied elves
This paradise, adorned with wolves.

Buffon did well, for children's eyes
Perceive what we cannot surmise.
They are pure dreamers; and the wise
Try to please those who fantasise.

Summer. Bright June. Like Eden's bowers,
This park is radiant with flowers;
I shall be there with Jean and George,
When Jean and George take me in charge.
We'll visit, with its growly bears,
This précis of the Universe.

I go because it's what Jean wants,
And against Jean I've no defence.
I have two depths in which to pry:
The child in trembling infancy,
And God, on fire to create:
The very sweet, the very great.
They blaze with but a single flame:
Vast star, small soul, one and the same.

In Buffon's park I get to know
Boorish baboon, brute buffalo,
And lumps and humps that do not please:
I learn to like God's fantasies.
May it please parson, monk, and bonze,
God works His wonders as He wants.
He has Nisard, who seems to be
Concierge at the Academy,
Clean up the waters of good taste;
Fills virgin woods with apes unchaste;
Makes Dupin dog-faced. (Dogs: poor fellows!)
India's Manichæans tell us
God's demon double solves the riddle,
And hell is heaven's filthy puddle;
Providence serves Necessity;
The cosmic insufficiency
Fails to fill up infinity;
Blind nature's law says evil would
Always make inroads into good.
Creation, then, displays anomalies,
And sometimes God proceeds by similes:
Immeasurable and abstruse,
He makes the buzzard, and the goose.
The critic's cage restricts the poet,
Who's tamed and tied and tethered to it:
When God creates, He's free to do it.
He has no boundary nor bourn,

Makes weeds spring up amidst the corn,
Pleads his star-badged immensity;
Drops fearsome vultures from the sky,
Sends horned contraptions by the dozen,
Goat, izard, snail, the auroch bison,
Wounding good sense, affronting reason;
We accept snakes, he snorts derision!
And when we joyfully appraise
His handiwork, and give due praise
To brindled tiger's golden eye,
To peacock's tailboard galaxy,
To antelope with orbs of blue,
To stately swan, what does he do?
Draws back a bolt in his barmy zoo,
Thrusts in our face the kangaroo!
God breaks, remakes, crops, nips and tucks,
Makes men the way he makes macaques,
Makes mole and lynx, revokes, retracts;
The popinjay who over-acts
Dwells with the bandit in one arbour:
The mandrill is the jaguar's neighbour;
The eagle with the parrot he
Installs, the brazen parody
Hitched to the epic poetry,
Both in one bush, to promenade
Through horrid jungle's light-and-shade.
Are we to laugh or be afraid?
We sense, within the shadow frayed
By golden beam or lightning-spear,
A death's-head, fading to a leer.
We can't set rules he must observe;
We must condone immoderate verve,
In such a poet! Need we glower,
If he, who tints the peach-tree's flower,
Bends rainbows on still seas, has gone
From humming-bird to mastodon?

His fun's to be in frightful taste:
Hydras on sea-beds, worms in the waste!
In all he does, he's a numero:
Rabelais' own Michelangelo.
He's God; I accept it.

Children too:
They are not sent to us to know,
From birth, the great world's ways. In nappies,
Our little treasures, when the sap is
Surging, are often rather rude:
This I'll admit. Amid the flood
Of cries and calls, the clop of leathers,
Bears with their keepers, bairns with their mothers,
Real live chimeras in my sight,
I gape at monster and at mite,
Deafened, as if by bees assailed,
That swarm at noon; I'm quizzed, I'm scaled,
Grandpa, apostle, both the same,
Enquiry desk and climbing-frame.
Noisy tots, baying beasts, noisome nests,
I pardon all; and this persists:
In the great echoing park I'm reconciled,
A man whom sunrise and the young make mild,
Glad of this double fire, well-warmed, beguiled,
Indulging God as I indulge the child.

ii. Animals Talk

Animals talk: yes, Dupont knows
Their songs, cries, rages, joys and woes.
Puss-in-Boots; Homer's wonderful horses;
Phaedrus, scribbling down the beasts' discourses;
La Fontaine in the long grass lying,
Watching from the undergrowth, dreaming, spying;
Æsop, thinker with a back like Pindus,
Heard them in Greece; Bidpai, on the Indus.
Twilight jargon of limpid lagoons
Revealed to Florian, officer of dragoons;
Bald-headed prophet Ezekiel
Was a wild man, listened to wild beasts as well.
Simple beasts have their dialogue:
Owl in the dark and croaking frog,
Growling bear and braying donkey,
Goose and turkey, mongoose and monkey,
Wasp that picks a quarrel with a bee:
Beasts have a human personality.

iii. What the Public Says

Five-year-old. Six-year-old.

Five. Lions are wolves.

Six. Animals are very naughty.

Five. Yes.

Six. Little birds are naughty and they're dirty.

Five. Yes.

Six (sees snakes) Snakes are...

Five (examines one) It's got skin! It's got skin on it!

Six. Watch out, the monkey's going to take your bonnet.

Five (sees tiger) Wolf!

Six. It's bear's bedtime soon, let's see the bear.

Five (sees bear) Pretty!

Six. He's climbed...

Five (sees elephant) Horns in his mouth! Look there!

Six. Elephant's big. I like him.

Seven-year-old (comes up and tugs them away from viewing the elephant) Come with me!
He'll hit you with his nozzle – can't you see?

iv. To George

Let's go, dear George, and see the Zoo:
'Jardin des Plantes', Big Top, wherever:
Off to Assyria! and we'll never
Leave Paris. Off to Timbuctoo!

Zebras and jackals and ounces; regal
Lions; the sly lynx, and the bear,
(Growl, growl) and that poetic pair,
Vulture of night and sun-drunk eagle;

Leopards from Nineveh and Tyre;
Boa constrictor, silent, feared,
And the great bird that grows a beard
And steals our sheep, the lammergeier;

The amphisbæna's there as well,
Job's two-faced friend, who smiles and lies;
And the black panther's fearsome eyes,
Two flaming holes that show us hell.

We'll watch in safety, at our ease,
Wing-beats of wild birds, near, not far;
Wolves and gazelles, a jaguar,
And lovely dazzling colibris.

Leave human hubbub. In the Park,
Look down, across the stifling murk,
Where sorrows pace, and check, and lurk,
And vaguely call from deepest dark.

They may not hear, they may not heed,
For beasts are shadows mazed in gloom.
Their cries are wild, their eyes flash doom;
Yet they affirm some lofty creed.

We monarchs, idly chattering,
Know nothing of the harm we do:
Truth comes, and we reject the true,
Against all reason reasoning.

The judge's robe, the bishop's sleeve,
Can't match the woods' wild animal.
Forests set free the dreaming soul:
In pews, I doubt; on peaks, believe.

God speaks in shadow-tones, obscure.
No Court can match the mountainside.
When Man has stood and speechified,
Go out and hear the lion's roar.

v. *God Again, up to a Point*

A lovely place, of elms' and cedars' whispers!
The donkey sings as if he'd seen Don Quixote;
The tiger is a regal anchorite,
The rhino and the hippo look a fright;
Idyllic dreams enrapture bibliophiles,
Who see old bores in yawning crocodiles.
Here, the baboon pays up to please Miss Monkey;
The scientist is studied by the donkey;
Vultures make eyes at owls. Wise men do best
To go and ponder, where the wild birds nest
In shady trees, and all appears at rest
And yet is wide awake, watching and waiting;
Refusal means consent; love comes out shooting:
And all can hear the breeze's gentle fluting.

So let's learn, love, and live – and let live – for the skies
Are immense; we'll be experts more witless than wise.
Let's give diligent ear to the infinite hum,
For it all tells a story, there's no deaf and dumb;
Let's see all that we can of the beasts: let's be taught:
Since all nature is dreaming, our role's to take thought.
Curiosity's rather like saying a prayer:
Man's as big at the front as he's small at the rear:
From Euclid to Newton, from Job to Pascal,
He's a peeper who wants to see over the wall:
Nature looks at our science and, fond of a laugh,
She appends her own flourish, the long-necked giraffe.
Take a look, for our spirit impels us; and cunning
Old God knows we're curious: he watches us, grinning.

It's said God has been criticised
As wild and over-energised,
As awkward, vast, and not to scale,
Having no nothingness at all.

Giants and dwarfs he makes profuse,
Practises prism and chasm abuse.
The sun is something out of Góngora:
Gargantuan lamp! Preposterous plethora!
Here is Sahara, there Siberia:
Discrepancies, disequilibria.
Contrast is rife: his Will be done:
The coal-black crow, the snow-white swan.
One day we freeze, the next we fry:
Raised eyebrows, at the Academy!
Why comets? Wherefore meteors?
The sober scientist abhors
Flashiness: he's dissatisfied:
The martinet cannot abide
God, nor the pedant: he provokes
And wearies science, with his jokes.
You start again, you never end,
Feel a snake sliding through your hand
With scales of sheer iridium;
'Enough!' you cry: there's more to come.

God is the people's friend, does more,
Gives flowers alike to rich and poor;
Knowing no limits, he purveys
His colours, lights, and flashing rays.
It hurts my eyes! the poppet cries:
It's all too much! And she is wise.

God shapes the world as he will, on its azure wings.
You soar, his lightning strikes; you browse, he stings,
Lacing with irony his epic thunder.
(Was Planche, the critic, stung? I shouldn't wonder!)

The wind's a failure, wittering mindless voice,
Inconsequential, inconclusive noise;
The ocean tends to get a swollen head.
Myself, I wonder what would have been said
Of God and all his wonder-works of plenty,
The weird and muddled whatnot of infinity,
The world he rules, the exaggerated skies,
The heaps of stars of every shape and size,
The way he crams them in the telescope,
By Voltaire's friends at the Café Procope.

vi. To Jean

I like the wild beasts too, I won't deny.
You they amuse, and me they edify.
It's surely by design that God displayed,
In these fierce heads, the jungles' light and shade.

Born to protest, to probe, and to believe,
I see the sneaking asp beneath the rose:
The flower fears not the serpent, but yet Eve
Must fear the fiend. I delve these sombre laws.

We give the earth our orders. We are kings,
Kings who ape monkeys, and are aped by them,
Be they our forebears or our crafted things.
Far down beneath our feet, in fateful gloom,

We, who some dark astonished world regards,
Have with our sometimes odious yoke subdued
The creeping monster and the haggard brute:
We are like fiends, they take us to be gods.

Strange laws and grim confusion! Has this earth
Seen the last fact, observed the final truth?
Might Venus give new apparitions birth,
Angels yet spring from fearsome Behemoth?

Mystic transfiguring! Gulfs and pinnacles!
The soul discards the body's dismal tatters.
Wretch made sublime! The same vile grub that crawls
Is the loved butterfly that freely flutters.

vii. Children and Animals

Youngsters in swarms, beneath the arching fronds!
For sure, these rows of statues and of ponds,
Straight-ruled parterres, this cedar-tree resigned,
That oak dogmatic Boileau might have signed,
Black cross-beams over scented flowers in bloom:
All these are Buffon's honorarium.
The Academician ran Lenôtre's comb
Through the uncivilised and scary locks
Of Pan, the god of thickets, heaths and rocks.
We want for nothing! Roses still exude
Scents and desires and love in plenitude;
Summer is no less summer; life retains
Its confidence; the rising sun attains
The zenith, no less radiant than before;
Children still play, and monstrous creatures roar.

Good joyful horror grips the little treasures.
'The animals!' they shout: 'Come on!' My pleasure's
Listening, drinking in each charming cry.
'Come on!' And off they run: what ecstasy!
They pause at cages where the bluebirds dream
Of migrant flight. 'What a big cat – d'you see him?'
'Ah, that's the tiger.' Bigger kids teach the young
To respect jackals, pythons, the orang;
And spout the names of bad old bears, malign,
Thought to have eaten soldiers of the line.

A monstrous sight! The dragon's gaze and jaws,
The scales and spurs and the protruding claws,
The lurid glow amid decaying trees;
Abysmal spectres, horrid reveries,
Real ones, seen by sad seers with troubled eyes
Beneath the dread transparency of seas:

Seen creeping through the nameless vilenesses
In the great yawning of the stunned abyss:
The hydra's grimly open sevenfold jaws,
A chaos! Dismal, pallid, merciless,
A stab at an existence, life's first try:
From which, the tongue-tied rage of jealousy!
That is the animal: that's what the child
Sees, wonders at, and fears, feeling a mild
Triumph: the child sees night, the beast sees dawn.
These roar and howl and gnash, dark teeming spawn;
While those are cherubs, trembling, frail, and cute,
Who go to see some beast in winter-white,
Or one whose eye is tropically bright.
These growl, hate, threaten, hiss and sting and bite:
The children feel quite safe, as Nurse is here:
When there's no danger, there's such fun in fear!
What grown-ups think, perhaps the young discover:
A king in his cave, a tiger in his Louvre:
Such pleasure. 'Nice and ugly! Come and see.'
A curious instinct: horror is enjoyed
By grace, that seeks out what it should avoid.
'This way! – No, that way! – Quick, come here! D'you see it?
Throw them your cake. – Not all of it! – Well, throw it!
I like the wolves. – The bears are best, I say!'
Laughter, and sun; and those born yesterday,
Still speechless in the din beneath the trees,
Are there mysterious, with great wide eyes,
Pondering.

Africa, impassable
Sand-seas and folds, horizons horrible,
Darfur, Dahomey, Lake Nagain, Sahara;
America, and India, where Ahura
Mazda the Zoroastrian god meets Homer,
Rough crossroads; moonscapes of the wild chimera,
Haunts of orang-utang with stick in hand,
Where nature's inhumane, insane, unplanned:

Jungles imagined in a fever-dream,
Vast plains, the swift incursion of a stream
Now swollen to a river, huge, unchained,
Where lions roar, amazed to be constrained
By fiercely rising floods on sudden isles,
Deserts whose black-clad monks are gavials,
Where boa constrictors dream and hold their breath,
Inert as fallen tree-trunks, plotting death:
You lands of baobabs, bamboos, lianas,
You know we have our Georges and Joannas:
Make monsters! Lakes and forests, use your crests,
Your nights, your noises: build us Moloch-beasts!
Chasms, stuff all your glories in their maws:
Give them your rocks to be their teeth and jaws,
Your hurricane their voice, their face your horror,
Give them the quality of pope and emperor;
Out from the bush, their palace and their stable,
Let all their joy leap forth insuperable!
The cassowary makes a splendid senator,
The pompous goose is magic, needs a mitre,
In Scaramouche God saw the chimpanzee:
I love the humming-bird, the colibri,
But, Nature, what I look for in your plans
Is boldness, Behemoths, Leviathans!
Babies emerge from twilit mystery:
They'd fret, if there were nothing here to see!
An outsize need for what's astonishing,
That's childhood: and with that in mind, I sing
In praise of Life's large-scale developments:
Great beasts are treasured by our innocents.
Breed! Multiply! To work, dread deities!
Deserts! Your perfumes and your botanies
Are sweet, but so are your monstrosities.
No question: hippos, rhinos, jumbos too,
Are made for little children and the zoo!

viii. Strange Feeling

Strange feeling for my soul
To see a babe in arms,
Flower not knowing winter,
Angel not knowing Satan,
Come softly to fierce Nature,
And rattle at the monster!
When seraphs bonny-blue
Come out of mystic sky
To roam the bible's pages,
No purer dawns their eye,
No saintlier their brow,
Than that of guiltless child
Chuckling at hellish creatures.

Black heaven! Mighty roar!
The beast, blind soul, face foaming,
Hurls far through hostile plain
Harsh cry, horrendous weapon.
Fraught depths of dark are howling:
Savage obscene Astarte,
Nature accursed and wretched,
African gulfs, Stymphalian
Birds, the Nemean Lion,
Fierce Atlas, Athos haunted
By countless claps of thunder
Like gnats on summer waters;
Pelion piled on Ossa,
The boar of Erymanthus
And the Lernæan hydra;
Grim Calydon, despairing.

The infant scans the shade, peers at the tawny lions.
The creature snarls: for whom, this furious defiance?
The infant burbles: can we say who it is calling?
Two voices intertwine, the sweet and the appalling.
The child is hope, the beast is hunger: both are states
Transitional: one foams and froths, one pipes and prates:
Each is intent, by some mysterious circumstance,
On saying what it knows, and getting what it wants.
Their tongues are tied, and struggling to undo the knot.
Do they accost each other? Querulous or cute,
Both try their best. The child is joyful, jovial:
Faced with the fearsome apparition rearing tall,
Mother and nanny near, the child takes charge of all.

Two beings: each from some dark place emerges:
One from the blue; the other from those orgies,
Couplings of dwarf and giant: dreadful kiss,
Called chaos, of the void and the abyss.
Their unclean cave, deep down beneath us all,
Thrusts to the light its bleary breathing-hole;
Chaos, black crashes, whirling hurricanes,
Spoiled elements turned into hooligans
In the great cess-pool, scourges, maladies,
All-rutting and all-mating madnesses,
Where All's made pregnant and produces Nil;
Beauty and Truth and Goodness swamped in Hell:
Hades of Orpheus, Homer's Erebus,
The Sphinx of Thebes with gaze imperious:
This is the evil, the demented deed,
Which, giving Chaos form, Creation made:
The venerable sun's assailed by shade,
Vile gulfs convulse, the unformed defies the ideal,
The avenging Fury bares her womb to Baal,
Dark forces gather, all escaped from hell;
Then lightning-flashes draw their swords in rage,

Death-knell of Janus and the Golden Age,
And Rhea, mother (if we trust the Mage)
Of beasts. The fearsome thing, with roars and belches,
Was spewed at dead of night from these debauches.

That's the scary monster. What about the youngster?

The child now, happy dreamer, reassuring, pure,
Is the reverse enigma, from the deep azure.
Every small bird, the sparrow, blue-tit, wagtail, warbler,
Each pert-voiced gossip-monger is the child's own brother.
Those woodland mites grow wings; meanwhile the childish soul
Thrives on the myrrh and cinnamon that perfume all
The blue; the interlacing blooms and radiant beams
Which, if we act aright, we witness in our dreams;
Obscure entanglement of noble forest-branches
In which the birds are God's own flights of angels;
The glow of light like water's clear reflecting
When trees turn upside-down in ponds at evening;
And living lilies, laughing skies, and lullabies:
These are the fresh-faced infant's latest memories.
It wakes on earth, bemused: it's just seen paradise,
Seen God. It has no terrors, does not recognise
Evil; no wolf, sea-eagle, tawny tiger, nor
The trickster fox, can frighten it; untouched by fear,
It sings. And what can ever be more touching for
Us thinkers than this trust in Heaven, pushed so far
As to come close up smiling to the depths of hell!
Angelic children! All, sin and the ocean swell,
Hydras that meres of evil tumble in their waves,
Claws that are fearsome jungles, jaws that are deadly caves,
Howls, growls and roars and rattles, apparitions, wild
Panics, the power of Satan, ravening, reviled,
All melt in deep blue innocence, before the child!

To gaze on Caliban, and still be Ariel;
To have a splendid sky within a humble soul,
That savage angry visions of the midnight crew
Can never harm; to feel so full of light, and so
Sweet, that their breath cannot snuff out one star in you!

I dream. I seem to hear a dialogue:
Grim tragedy and pastoral eclogue,
Horror and love. Neither shines bright with dawn.
The child, it seems, has something to explain;
The monster snarls, and, stooping to the rose,
Gives ear. Great heaven! Who can tell, who knows
What babbler may to bellower disclose?

Some secret... All attend with thoughtful ear:
The graceful blossom and the graceless briar;
All is alert, all vibrant, all a-quiver,
Thicket and leafy branch and breeze and river,
In twilight's dappled half-obscurities
That witnessed once the fights of Hercules,
Flights of Bellerophon, great prophecy
By sublime Amos of a world to be!
We feel some sacred, undefined emotion
For Nature, God's continuing creation,
And the whole mystery: a tenderness,
As if we saw the daybreak's rays of peace
Rise above shapeless headlands, when the clean,
And pure, address the impure and obscene.

ix. *The Wild Beast's Face*

The wild beast's face is frightening: we feel
The undeciphered riddle that we call
Nature: it's dazzling, dismal, and unknown:
Dark quest, yoke, slavery, rebellion:
The awesome face and presence of the lion.
Discordant, stormy, wild, it isn't free:
What's the strange balance – O monstrosity! –
Splendour and horror of a universe
That's ruled by God, with Satan the inverse?
Where stars, a luminous and livid crowd,
Seem to be captive, fleeing through the void,
And thrown at hazard, as a dice is thrown,
Always chained up, and always on the run?
What is this fearsome holy miracle
Of seeing Paradise and sensing Hell?
What is this dread, when hopes are put to flight,
Of endless suns eclipsed in endless night,
God vanished in the brute without a trace?
When they behold the monster face to face,
The backwoods dreamers crazed with second sight,
Pale prophets who hear voices, all intuit
Something enormous in the animal,
Sensing, in that dark head's embittered snarl,
The lowest depths, uneasy at their gaze,
The everlasting mystery that stays
Secretive, not to be invaded by
Pale solitaries' curiosity.
These are the men the sombre shade reveres;
They sense the sphinx's anger, and their hairs
Stand stiff on end, strange fears assault their brains.
The monster frowns: blood freezes in their veins!

x. That Old Idea

All kinds of children, fair, dark, red,
Who safely sleep at night in bed
With the blue heavens in their head,
Throng, where the savage beasts are penned.
They see the naked element,
Down deep! – the snake's entanglement,
Fierce dragon, jackass, pard with beard,
Jackal from whom thc ghosts run scared,
Spectral gorillas, lawless wolves,
Lynxes, who once enjoyed themselves
As friends of some Ezekiel,
A toiling seer, with truth to tell;
This proud exile, that convict vile...
They snarl, these hoarded captives, while
The little shining charmers smile.

Growls down below! They smile, admire
Abysmal cries of monsters dire:
They sing, they swarm, like sunbeams borne
On wings, and thrill us like the dawn
In Virgil's fields. Their glees engage
With bellows of revolt and rage
From vultures' jail and lions' cage.

The children's smiles don't fade. Confronted
By sweetness humble and unstinted,
Natural, not to be denied,
We are astonished, stupefied;
Orpheus and Japhet come to mind;
Job, Thales, Epicurus wind
A spiral of dark vertigo;
We seem to slither down, and go
Groping for someone down a well:
The soul may ask, and God might tell.

Could it perhaps be true, that old idea?
The restless Magi dreamed it in Chaldea;
Pythagoras surmised it, Hermes too.
Could the wild notion be profoundly true:
Might every savage beast be – Tantalus?
Could this be fact, tremendous, ominous:
That serpents, wolves, gorillas, all non-humans
Are sombre masks concealing unseen demons?
These terrifying creatures of the dark,
Tigers and vipers, flattened skulls that lurk,
Vile brows crushed by the heel of their creator,
The boa constrictor and the alligator,
Prehensile monkeys and black brooding bears:
Convulsive scowls, brute instincts, crazy stares
That flout our reason: these, grim avatars
In jungles; those, that hide and float and flee
Through the shot silk and pearl-shine of the sea;
The grubs, the ghosts, the woods' menagerie,
Live creatures in the tomb of dreadful night,
Phantoms whose only law is appetite –
Great heavens! Can they be the ones we name
'The damned', still expiating deeds of shame
Committed in a human life that's past,
Their eyes still smitten by a thunder-blast,
Still gibbering with hate and dread? They tell –
For this they come amongst us – tales of hell,
Vainly attempting to express their anguish
In the brute bellow of a bestial language,
Convicts who snarl and roar and groan and yowl,
Blind in the lurid blaze, who speechless howl,
Naked beneath their iron destiny,
Pondering hell for ever – can it be?
Nature's sad losers, banned from clemency,
Forever hopeless, they may think, and see
Sun after sun go down… Then suddenly,
When all is crushed and broken utterly,

All hope foregone, fled, vanished, and denied
To beings both depraved and terrified –
What an astonishment, what joy to hear
These innocent young voices lilting near!
Someone! but who? Who spoke? Perplexity!
Pure light pervades the dismal masonry
That shadow-images have flickered on:
Leviathan encounters Halcyon!
The Flood beholds the Dove! The cradle's bloom
Diffuses, penetrating through the tomb,
Bathing the damned in kindly light of morn.
They are not hated by the newly-born!
Her sombre toils great spider Fate unbars!
How bright are children's eyes, ye sainted stars!
If we can enter, we can exit too:
All is not lost! A message from the blue!
Heaven's more heavenly in those sweet eyes!
When God descends from the eternal skies
To sad and dismal earth, let him proceed
By way of childhood! Then he's God indeed.
The roof above us opens, and we see
Hope born again, the impossibility.
Never again to bite, never to growl!
How can we guess what happens in the skull
Of beasts, both feared and fearing? Who can tell?
Light in the depths! An angel intervenes!
Hell's burning torment in the grim ravines
Is suddenly assuaged by innocence,
Pure as a dewdrop, in a childish glance!
Eyes shining, footsteps pattering! What chance
These monsters think, and talk, when night comes on,
Dumbfounded at the unfamiliar dawn
That breaks along the harsh severe horizon?
They sense the holy thrill of timeless pardon;
They seem to feel the shedding of their chains;
Sober reflection smoothes their matted manes;

Hell is less black and ruinous; the eye,
Now milder, of these captives seems to spy,
In pure half-light made blue by distant sky,
A temple's shade beside their hovel rising.
Hell finished! Darkness listening to reason!
Mercy and light in the enormous prison!
Their hearts are strange: who knows what hopes beguile…

But oh, what promise, when the angels smile!

V Jean Asleep – II

She sleeps: those eyes will shine when day has dawned.
Clutched in the dark, my finger fills her hand:
Careful she shouldn't waken, I peruse
High-minded journals, all of which abuse
My name: one wants my readers certified;
One wants my twisted works by fire destroyed;
Another – and the tears bedew its eye –
Would have me stoned by every passer-by;
My writings are a dismal toxic pile
Where Evil's pitch-black dragons writhe and coil;
One pious paper says I'm sent from hell;
I'm Antichrist, I'm Satan; you may well
Avoid me in dark corners! Here's an offer
Of hemlock – 'Drink it!' I burnt down the Louvre,
I killed the hostages, caused mobs to rave
For share-outs; Paris burns; my features have
The red of shame, for I'm the arsonist;
Assassin, miser, cut-throat: quite a list!
I might have been less sombre, and less sinister,
If He-Who-Reigns had deigned to make me Minister.
I am the poisoner, the man of blood...
So they insult me, and their voices flood,
Unceasing, unrelenting, round my head.
And the child sleeps, and dreams, as if she said:
Calm, dear old father, calm and clemency! –
Holding my hand, and squeezing, peacefully.

VI Old Age and Youth Together

i. My Spirit is so Made

My spirit is so made that there's no man,
Nor any notion whatsoever, can
Alarm it. I've no sacred master-plan;
I've spurned the sophist, pulled the tyrant's beard;
Not being covetous, I'm not afeared;
Unquenched by fright, only by honour stirred.
Sclerotic, lofty, ponderous as a rock,
I cannot easily be driven back,
Scared off, nor pleasurably coaxed ahead;
Force I resist, by pleas I may be swayed,
But earthly benefits do not persuade.
Friends, I declare that I am satisfied,
That my supreme ambition's not denied:
I am repaid; the gods in mercy gave
Fulfilment of my vows in life. I crave
No Trajan's column, no plinth Olympian,
As long as I'm assured the smile of Jeanne.

ii. Cradle Song

I'm watching, awake. Have no fear – I'll stay till you sleep.
The angels shall come and their lips shall touch your head:
And over you I desire no dream shall creep
Of dread.

I desire that seeing you here, with your hand in mine,
The wind shall sound not the storm but the sweet-voiced viol,
And that, stealing over your sleep, the night malign
Shall smile.

Above each tremulous cradle the poet leans,
And murmurs sweet and low, where the babe reposes:
He is their lover, and sings them cantilenes
Like roses.

He is purer than April that balms the grass-fringed trees,
And May when the small birds peck at the basket's brim:
His voice is a thrill in the soul; the very bees
Envy him.

He adores these nests of lace and of silken stuff;
In the spotless home there's a gaiety that cheers
His heart with bursts of laughter, and sweetness enough
For tears.

He's the goodman, the sower who sows the freshness of joys;
He laughs. But, come the kings and all their claque
Of slaves, if he sees the tigress's glittering eyes
In the dark,

If he sees emerge from Vienna, Berlin or Rome,
A lying-in-wait, an invasion, a catechism,
He rears erect, which is all he needs to become
An exorcism.

If he sees the vulture Bismarck or basilisk Rome
Or scheming spider Ignatius commit their crime,
He growls, he senses with anger the surge of doom
In his rhyme.

So much for the songs. The future he extols,
The insolence of the kings, and the peoples' right,
Are like a whirling tempest, in which his soul
Takes flight.

He comes running. France, to thy former pride return!
Deliverance! And they see him, the man, arise,
With God in his heart and the sword-blade's dazzle and burn
In his eyes.

And his thought, that ranges and roves, like mighty keels
On the wave, like banners in black war-tumult ringed,
Is a measureless chariot of the dawn, whose wheels
Are winged.

iii. The Scar

The scar has formed an ugly, scabby crust:
Jean picks it, makes it bleed, because she must.
She shows the tattered finger. "Look – I just
Took the skin off it, off my nasty place."
I scold: she cries: I see her tearful face:
I'm crushed. "Let's make it up, Jean. I give in:
Give me a smile and we'll be friends again."
The sweet child hugs me, safe in my caress,
Announcing, with that consummate largesse,
"I love you – I won't hurt myself again."
Such tender ecstasy! We're both in heaven,
She from my lenience, me from being forgiven.

iv. A Punch

A great big punch, thrown by the little hand.
"What's this, then! Tell her off! She hit you, Grand-
Papa! And you look fonder than before!"
"Rebuke?" say I: "Can't do it any more!"
I ask you! Nothing but my smile remains:
I have seen Judas' treason, Nero's bans,
Triumphs of Satan and the evil shades;
Poured out my deepest heart in ill-starred rage;
I've seen the church connive at wickedness,
Bishops obey, the clergy acquiesce;
I have stood roaring on the rocky crest:
Against the gross assault of the barbarian
And the black curses belched out by Napoleon,
Against the murder of our laws and virtues,
Paris without Barbès, Rome without Brutus;
France shipwrecked, Caesar buoyant; both deploring,
I've sent my great sepulchral verses soaring.

Our dungeon's vault was sealed: I made it move,
Turned loose the hurricanoes up above,
Oaths, lightning-flashes and the hue-and-cry
In sacred caverns of the cloudy sky;
In days that seemed like nights I have unfurled
All the sad voices of the underworld,
Laments, tears, threnodies for France betrayed:
Juvenal, and Isaiah, a darker shade;
Iambic maledictions, obloquies
That crash like rocks of hatred in the skies;
Chastised the dead themselves beyond the grave,
Punished the eagle to avenge the dove,
Lashed Nimrod, Caesar, and Napoleon,
Called to account the very Pantheon,
Shaken at times that lofty portico;
Dealt justice on the earth, and down below;
Cleansed the foul vapours from the distant sky.
One comes home rather weary, certainly;
One isn't cross with small familiar flies,
Or little chicks that peck in henneries,
Or gentle twitting from melodious nests.
Our infant deities, infernal pests,
Moppets and monkeys, fascinate: they bite,
And we hear songs. Peace has this requisite:
Forgiveness. Be severe, be Cato or Dante,
Not for the little, only for the mighty.
Are we to shout against their fledgling murmur?
For sparrows, do we buckle on our armour?
Do we fight off the sunrise? It's absurd!
The Thunder in his home is seen, not heard.

v. *I'm Pleasantly…*

I'm pleasantly lunatic over my Jean.
Because she's a woman she feels like a queen.
She knows all their tricks: to be shining-limbed beauties,
To quell with a look those who shrink from their duties,
To know with mere posies and chiffons and smiles
How to fathom and dazzle the hearts she beguiles;
With a man who's cantankerous, grim, and morose,
She is sweet as the sky, she out-roses the rose;
At the ripe age of three she has mastered it all:
She's the beautiful flower on my tumbledown wall,
My sweet special study, my sprig and my spree;
When my rhymes importune with a beggarly plea,
She throws them a sunbeam; a child for all that,
She's already bedecked with magnificent hat,
An eye-catching dress, scarlet shoes on her feet;
She moves with the mayfly's irregular beat,
A woman, in ribbons of azure or green,
Neat and fresh, as her spirit is pure and serene.
She is heavenly by right, she is lovely by role,
She has come to her throne and befuddled my soul.

vi. The Pot of Jam

Jean was shut in the dark on bread and water,
For some offence. Not doing what I ought to,
I broke the ban, dropped by her, 'on the lam',
And slipped her a clandestine pot of jam,
Outside the law. All those who, in my town,
See that the general good is not done down,
Saw red. Jean's voice was sweetly modulated.
"I shall not thumb my nose again," she stated;
"I won't make Pussy scratch me." Uproar. "Look!"
They cried. "That child can read you like a book!
She knows how weak and wet you are. She's seen
The way you laugh whenever there's a scene.
How can we govern her? You overthrow
Discipline, every time. The rules just go
For nothing. Standards fall, the reins are slack.
You ruin things. What's left to hold her back?"
I hung my head and said: "I've no reply.
I'm in the wrong. This is the laxity
That's always ushered peoples to their doom.
Put me on dry bread in a darkened room."
"You've earned it, and we'll do it." Closeted,
Jean raised her lovely eyes to me, and said,
Serene as any dear sweet-natured lamb,
"All right, I'm going to bring you pots of jam."

vii. Song to make Little Children Dance in a Ring

In the oleander-shade,
Dancing to the tambourine,
Talk low-voiced and unafraid
Jacqueline and Jack the Lad,
Jack the Lad and Jacqueline.

Join at dusk the merry scene,
Dance, with lusty serenade:
No devotions vespertine!
Jacqueline and Jack the Lad,
Jack the Lad and Jacqueline.

Tree along the shore marine
Carved as if by burin-blade,
Black beneath a sky serene.
Jacqueline and Jack the Lad,
Jack the Lad and Jacqueline.

Wicked wolf is in the glade.
Sparrow hears the sermon said,
Sees him gobble up the grain.
Jacqueline and Jack the Lad,
Jack the Lad and Jacqueline.

Watercress and rose-marine:
Sniff them out, you leveret,
Champ the grasses, blade on blade.
Jacqueline and Jack the Lad,
Jack the Lad and Jacqueline.

In the elms, the bold young bard
Floats a quatrain: 'Yours to win,
With a kiss, Red-Riding-Hood.'
Jacqueline and Jack the Lad,
Jack the Lad and Jacqueline.

There's a dell that isn't seen.
Coach and horses in the glade
Sound a light fanfaronnade!
Jacqueline and Jack the Lad,
Jack the Lad and Jacqueline.

viii. The Broken Vase

Heavens! All China shattered on the ground!
This vase, pale, soft, vague image on a pond,
Covered with birds, flowers, fruits, and the untrue
Unformed abstractions of the drowsy blue:
This curious, fat, unique, uncanny one,
Vessel of moonlight in the midday sun,
That seemed alive, with bright fire shining in it,
That seemed almost a beast, almost a spirit:
Mariette was doing the bedroom and she knocked it
By mistake with her elbow, and (there now!) crocked it.
That roundness, full of dreamlike images –
Cattle of gold, on porcelain pastures grazing –
I loved it, bought it somewhere on the Quays:
The young would contemplate my explanation.
'This is the yak; here's the four-handed monkey;
This is a learned doctor, or a donkey:
He's saying pious words. No, just a yawn.
Here is a mandarin, a temple man:
Look at that paunch: a great big expert, then!
Look at this. Here's the tiger in his den,

The owl's in his hole, the king's in his high hall;
The devil's in his hell, not nice at all!'
Creatures delight us: any youngster feasts
On the enchanting magic of wild beasts.
I really liked this vase, then. Now, it's dead.
I came in, furious, fierce, and loudly said:
'So! Who's done this?' Brusque entry, you'll agree.
So Jean, who saw that Mariette was shaken,
Who saw my fury and her consternation,
Threw me an angel's glance and answered 'Me'.

ix. And She Told Mariette

And she told Mariette: 'I was perfectly sure
If I said it was me, he would say nothing more.
I'm not scared of him: he's just my grandfather:
He hasn't the time to get into a lather:
He's never that angry, because he forever
Must look at the flowers, and say in hot weather:
"Wear a hat on your head when you go in the sun;
Never haul the dog back by his collar, but run;
Don't trip over the steps, don't be stung by the bees,
Don't go bump on the marble's sharp corners. Now, please,
Time to play." And he vanishes into the trees.'

x. *Forgiving All*

"Forgiving all's a step too far;
Just giving all is more than par."
Well, I give all, and I forgive
All, to the young; and you misgive,
And sternly scold me: "Leniency
Is a bad model: amnesty
At home puts all in jeopardy.
Absolving faults committed by
The chubby-fingered, bright of eye,
The young and pure, is shocking, fearful.
If it caught on, why, what the devil!
This much we owe society:
A fatherly ferocity.
The sceptre's partner is the truncheon;
The palace basement is the dungeon.
Good works? An iron fist works well.
Would you be God, and have no hell?"
"Almost. Could I be unconcerned,
I ask you, if my children burned?
Well, no. Lord, no! and, *mea culpa*,
Rather than Yahweh, I'd be grandpa.
So, no religion? You are right.
Gangs clad in wolf-skins? Troglodyte,
Back to the cave? No, I'd eschew
The jealous God, and serve the true:
Return to pristine innocence,
To reason and to radiance!"
"You're crazy, grand-papa." Quite right.
Listen, you men of power and might:
Beware of me. I'm short on vengeance:
New to the game, I'm all indulgence,
Prefer young dawn to wintry cold,
A contrite lawgiver, grown old,

Who blames but never damns: for Jeanne
Has trampled down this mighty man,
Unsure of knowledge, prone to doubt,
Inclined to shelter souls without
Fireside and home; I rate despised
Sinners above crooks idolised,
Abiding those of no abode.
Don't raise me to the rank of God!
I'd do mad things: I'd laugh, and care
For roses, underdogs, the fair,
The scared, the weak: like soft white hair,
My rays would stream out everywhere.
With my colossal sprinkler I'd
Grow countless flowers on every side,
Quench at long range the fires of hell,
And make my orders clear as well;
I'd hide the stag, when hounds pursue;
If tyrants took me as their cue,
I'd say: No tyrants! Joy to all!
Pure hearts would be my miracle:
No wars at all. – No floods. – No scourges;
Believer-priests, and righteous judges.
As God, my hair would be a fog,
So cool, I'd seldom lose my rag,
Or disarrange my cloud of vapour,
Vexed by some youngster's misbehaviour.
I wouldn't make the shiners bright
Plunge headlong off the drapes of night,
Having no wish to add to Baruch
Spinoza's hassles with Sir Isaac
Newton. I would invite Voltaire
To dinner; Jesus would be there.
(Veuillot won't care for this at all:
Wait for his editorial!)

I'd have my finest wine, alas,
Poured by the friend of Lazarus
To serve the friend of John Calas;
My Eden would be generous,
With running water numinous
And soft, to cleanse the Syllabus;
I'd tell the kings: You're out of order!
Go! – With a wink I'd give the poor their
Pittance, and not a word to Peter,
And slit his saddlebags, that teeter
With heaps of gold called Peter's Pence.
I'd tell the Bishop of Orleans:
Reverend Father, you'd upgrade
Your Joan, you'd sanctify the Maid
Like the pure Virgin! Dupanloup,
Your zeal's excessive. Peace on you!
Were I Jehovah, what would please
Me more: a people on their knees,
Or men, erect, head high? Yes, these.
I'd pardon every last offence
With: Mind you guard your innocence;
I would demand, not frankincense,
But virtue, of the priests. I would
Be rational; if I were God,
I'd be a man whose deeds were good.

VII The Immaculate Conception

O holy Virgin, conceived without sin – (Christian prayer)

Everywhere, children. At the Tuileries.
Assorted Jeans and Georges and Maries;
One feeding, one asleep; a nightingale;
An older one who dreams of Grand Guignol;
A girl whose teeth attempt an apple-rind;
All the delightful morning of mankind;
Daybreak with Mr Punch; run, laugh and chatter;
A word with Dolly, who is quite a character;
Cream-cakes and skipping-ropes. I'm called on for
A charitable penny for the poor;
I give a pound. Oh, thank you, grandpa. Thanks!
Back to the game, to climbing, song and dance:
Blue skies! You be the horse. Now pull the cart.
I'm coachman. Left. Right. Whoa there! We could start
Puss-in-the-corner. Blind man's buff, maybe.
The old man's warmed by their simplicity
Around his bench. They murmur and repeat:
Their limbs are ruddy and their breath is sweet
As roses in the deep ravines in May;
Their fine hair shimmers with the rising day.
It's all so charming... All so *execrable*!
It's Sin!

Look in our missals, read our bible,
Read Abbé Pluche, read Trublet's notes on Paul,
Veuillot, whatever counts on earth at all...
Just one conception is immaculate:
All cradles but the starry crib are dirt,
Marriage the foul four-poster of the pit.
When man says Love, the heavens answer Sin!
All's filth, and atheists dissent, alone;

All women shameful, all except for one.
So all these children are malfeasances!
Bird, do you build your nest? How wrong that is!
Over the sweet brood, scheming darkness leers:
God winks his eye at Satan, tells him: Here's
Something for you: this guiltless girl or boy:
My crime! And so this gust of life and joy,
Childhood, this whirling swarm of souls that's sent
By April love, a spreading wonderment,
These angel-constellations in our night,
Sweet lips, dear heads, eyes full of limpid light,
Feet pattering on grass, the lovely din
Filling all space, welcomed by smiling sun:
All this is monstrous, pullulating Sin!
Evil! The error's in the newly-born!
O wretched clergy! O unholy scorn!

In the great sunrise, priests are sunk in gloom:
They trail the shadowy Fall, the formless doom.
Black night is in their dogmas' folds. The couple
Is in the wrong; the fruit is despicable;
The seed is toxic. Children soil their mothers.
Life is a crime: these men are here to judge us.
No marriage-bed, not their own birth, is pure,
Not their own altar. What discomfiture!
Women, they write dire qualms across your brows:
One is enthroned, the rest are scandalous.
Madness! It's theirs, the disobedience:
Who knows what spittle's mixed in their incense?
They cry anathema. Profound offence:
The tree in flower, the dawn on fire, the soul at feast,
The seeing eye, the loving heart: all these are cursed:
More, the great endless joy of God, who cries
'I am the Father!' as he multiplies
Children on earth, and stars across the skies.

VIII Schoolboy Scribbles

Charles took his schoolbook and did some sketching.
The lesson was tiresome and the pen was itching,
The child couldn't put it away in peace
Till he'd done this enormous masterpiece.
All over the book are impromptu frescoes,
Same as the Alhambra's, hispano-morescos.
Inkblots looking like animals and birds
Swallow the sentences and gnaw at the words.
The text is all eaten, the margins come close,
And floating in the middle is the schoolmaster's nose.
Touching-up old Juvenal, the Latin lord of raillery,
Whose artistry satirical put Rome in the pillory,
On Caesar and Brutus and the high points of history
Charles puts his messy indecipherable mystery.
The giddy-goat of whimsy has clambered on the verse,
The book is prim and proper but the pupil is perverse:
His fun and his mischief blend with the emotions
Of Juvenal, the vengeful, running to the Russians.
The creatures are weird, thick, deep and monstrous,
Perched alike on Nero and on good king Codrus;
Inkblots nest in the elegant branches,
Ravaging the rhetoric, spoiling spondees.
A donkey, with a face like Nisard, brays,
Turns into an owl in the woods' dark ways;
Caught in the rain from a spilling inkwell,
Over his drenched head he's holding a dactyl.
All of it's the work of a dreamer's hand:
That's why the lad sends the swarming band
Of scrawls, immune to literary pleasure,
Winging through the gloom of the six-foot measure.
A game, and a dream! Can a juvenile,
Meshing with the poem, add a touch of style,
Glossing the masterpiece? A harmony:

Genius completed by naivety.
On the giant's shoulder, the child sits and plays.
Charles creates a flower, protruding from a phrase;
Sends a flying goblin through the rhythmic bushes:
The poem is shocked and it shakes and blushes.
A circle fills a page. Is it a dome? An egg? A box?
Out comes a weasel, that might be an ox.
The doodle is king of every line, imposing
Varieties of vegetable metamorphosing.
Charles has made the Latin generate a jungle.
Boredom and the random, buffoonery and bungle,
Squat this old text like a strange-looking structure,
Building a secondary architecture.
His ink brings night to the book's star-spangle.
And yet, just for moments, all the thick black tangle
Lines up its leafy boughs and colonnaded stoas,
Lets through your free ideas, to goggle at the stars.

This is the way that Charles has treated
The rugged old monument: he has plaited
Ivy on the rusting bronze, filled in
The titan's mask with a lunatic grin.
How he enjoyed it. A schoolboy pleasure!
Make the proud genius a household creature!
Live with the lion as one lives with a poodle,
Kennel up the pedants in their sad, squalid muddle!
Gleefully, artfully, beautify
The product of the School Book Company!
Skip-a-poem! Feet together, jump right across!
Charles is pleased with his master-class,
Bird on a lime-twig, preening in the glass.

Someone is watching, a man of absolutes.
Glazed eyes a-glint now with horrid impositions,
Glum mouth-corners where he hides in the volutes

The law and the prophets and the regulations,
Grammar-books and primers, half-days refused,
Self-important fury of a text-book abused.
Childhood is for flowers: we give a stone instead.
Here comes the Censor, the Deputy Head,
Gives the volume a disdainful look:
"Right. Disrespect for your set study book.
One thousand lines, on the spot." Papillon!
Devil's Island! The Castle of Chillon!
Nine years old, and he's missing all the fun:
Tantalus, Enceladus, and Ixion!
Seeing others play, he himself is banned,
Cranking out his punishment with failing hand.
Cloudless skies! Boring! He sighs with dread:
A thousand-line mountain looms overhead.
Charles is distraught. No swinging on the bars!
Copying Latin! These are barbarous shores!
Now is the hour of the hop, hop, hops;
The air is warm, there's greenness in the copse;
Sitting on the grass, while the white-throat laves
His feathers, at noon, in the clear spring's waves;
Cricket in the corn sings. A right to the meadows:
Rights of the child. Charles dreams, in the shadows
Of the book that's all daubed black with his crimes;
Dejected, seems to hear the droning rhymes
Of a Boileau, opening and yawning beside him.
Such a pile of books must have sorely tried him.
But there's no remorse, and he feels no shame,
His head's held high, he can see no blame.
Am I a criminal? Am I in the slammer?
Slave of the villains who conspired to write the grammar?
What have I done, then? The hour of play is gone:
Alone and abandoned! The tears begin to run.
He looks at the paper and he's in despair:
Copy, copy, copy, till a thousand lines are there!

Pedant! From the wood where the satyrs flute,
This is what you bring to your institute.
Tyrant, when you're spoken to, your frontal ridge
Puckers like a wave at an old arched bridge.
Children roused to anger, long years before now,
Devised for this labour the three-bladed plough.
'Come! Let us trick these contemptible men.'
And fiercely he seizes his triple-barrelled pen.
Out of the book comes a shade, or a soul,
Or a man. 'Fear not, child. I'm Juvenal.
I'm good; it's grown-ups that I terrify.'
Charles lifts his tear-filled eyes, says 'I
Am not afraid,' and the man marmoreal
Speaks above the background noise arboreal,
Above the childish frolic and insouciance:
'My boy, like you I was exiled once:
Just like you, I had scrawled some figures;
You annoyed the pedants, I annoyed the augurs.
Pupil of the envied Charlemagne College,
Show me your book!' And he looks at an image
With not much tail, and not a lot of head.
'What's that?' 'Sir, it's an animal,' he said.
'Ah, you put animals among my verses.
And why not, if God, in the shadows, disperses
Beasts through the forests and the sacred seas?'
Turning the pages intently, he sees –
'What's this? Splendid, despite the crooked line.'
'A nice little man, sir.' 'A nice one? Fine!
Just what was needed. My book overflows
With villains, and a nice one, among all those,
Gives pleasure. (You puffed-up Caesars – 'shun! –
This chappie is a god.) Many thanks, my son.'
With sovereign fingers through the pages he goes:
Nisard, the donkey, the schoolmaster's nose,
The weasel like an ox, and the mythical creature,

Inkblots with wings on, meshing with the metre:
All this merriment, scattered on his fury.
Juvenal is dazzled, shouts: 'This is very funny!'

Two souls in harmony, big and little sister,
Chatter and play; and the Sub-Magister,
Dark as midnight and cold as December,
Would hear all amazed, if he came to the chamber,
Under the College's stifling ceiling,
Old poet, sweet child, two laughs pealing.

IX Grandpa's Childhood Frolics (1811)

Pepita

With hairnet and *mantilla*, so
That rhyme took time to fit her,
(Could she be *Inesilla*? No!)
She proved to be Pepita.

Sixteen, a beauty, in her prime,
A buxom *señorita*...
Whatever the preceding rhyme,
The end-rhyme was Pepita.

Pepita... Yes! The good times past:
Victorious. I remember!
It all comes flooding in so fast,
Like rip-tides in November,

When waves return the bladder-wrack
And roll the stony cullet.
An escort watched my father's back,
A palace was our billet.

In Spain, in my beloved Spain,
O spring, O dawn so distant!
Aged eight, I was Pepita's swain,
Though close to non-existent.

"My name is Pepa, boy:" (she spoke)
"My father is a *grande*."
Amongst a folk beneath our yoke,
I thought myself a dandy.

Now Pepa stockpiled gold doubloons
Inside her silken hairnet;
And flames and joy and suchlike boons
Sprayed from her flaxen barnet.

Her watered silk from heels to hips,
Bolero jacket, *bolas*,
Blue velvet, jet-black lacy bits,
Danced in an aureolus.

Pepita, those were woman's charms!
She needed no exertion.
Crushed by the velvet on her arms,
My soul embraced coercion.

My heart was like a menaced nest,
And fluttered in her chamber.
A rose bouquet was on her breast,
Her necklace was of amber.

Each day a whining pantaloon
Came begging for a pittance;
At the same time, a bold dragoon
Contrived to gain admittance.

The crumbling dotard asked for alms
In croaking self-abasement,
While the resplendent man-at-arms
Swaggered beneath the casement.

Amber and roses! As I live,
She bowed her eleganza,
And gave the poor man his, to give
The soldier his, bonanza.

Away they went, the swell more proud,
Less pitiful the codger;
On him a groat had been bestowed,
A glance upon the soldier.

I hovered at the window's edge,
Too small to see, and trembling:
Smitten beyond my means to gauge,
Foolish beyond dissembling.

Said she with a coquette's élan,
"O let our troth be plighted!"
The soldier was her fancy-man,
Her spouse, the boy benighted.

I made a nincompoop's remark.
"Pipe down! Pipe down!" she pleaded.
Her dousing only fanned my spark!
The while this sport proceeded,

The troopers played at dominoes
And drank their toledano
In painted rooms and patios,
Palacio Masserano.

X Children, Birds and Flowers

i. A Group of Lads

I like a group of lads who gather, full of fun.
They mostly have fair hair, and the morning sun,
Going higher, gently touches them with gold.
When Roland, who plans and pledges, was not very old,
After the fencing-lessons and squad-parades
He used to play in the fields with his young comrades,
Idle Raymond and John from Pau: they formed a happy
Trio. One day the monk who ran the abbey
Passed by with his cross, and asked 'My children, what
Do you like, most of all, to see being torn apart?'
'A rare red steak,' says Raymond. 'A book,' says John from Pau.
'A flag' says Roland, summoning the battles of long ago.

ii. I am the Forester

I am the forester, day by day;
I am the gardener of the wild.
To me when autumn leaves are piled
The swallow whispers: Let's away.

Frost and snow turned sixty days:
On the woodland glades I call,
And the tender shoots, in case
They need anything at all.

Grow, you virgin briars! Wild thyme,
Hear me too: pour out your balm!
All you flowers beside the stream,
Diligently braid your hem!

I oversee, through half-closed door,
The wind that blusters on the heights,
Because he is a practised liar,
Fails to deliver, palters, cheats.

April deals with January,
Urgent measures are in place.
Anything diversionary?
I arrive at dawn, in case.

All things pass, yet start again:
I observe it with a passion,
All the great rejuvenation
That the darkness shirks in vain.

Brambles, ivies, lichens red,
How I love them, every one,
On a crumbling ruin's head,
Styles created by the sun.

When May-time flaunts her artistry
Along the bailey's dismal walls,
I tell these old unteachables:
"Make the spring welcome, set her free."

iii. In the Garden

I'm watching George and Jean. Black stormy sky
Turns pink, then bright: they play contentedly.
Beautiful days! Spring presses its advance,
Everything's green, the forest-frond enchants;
It's quite theatrical, the changing view.
What name for this sweet month appeals to you?
It's floral May, the noble marriage-bed
Of frailty and the boundless: nests are wed

To blue expanses, blades of grass to sky:
Everything's conscious of eternity:
It's dazzlement, it's hope, it's drunkenness:
Each plant's a woman, my verse a caress:
The gladiolus and convolvulus
Avenge the poets for our hideous
Bleak winter, while the periwinkle pays
All April's debt to January days.
April and May, be bold! Shine, lovely Sun,
And give us warmth! Almighty God, well done!
Spring never bankrupts us. The season passes
Like daybreak, sowing every road with roses.
Flame! Shadow! All is eerie, full of eyes;
Everywhere radiance, and mysteries!
Why does the halcyon scour the stormy wave?
For love. The chirping nest, the champing cave!
If lions ponder nature, wedlock, love,
What's man to be ashamed or fearful of?
Life opens every prison. Every chain
That starts in metal cruelty and pain,
Ends in sweet roses with the lily twined:
First we find hatred, heinous wars; we find
Tyrants and torture; then comes womankind!
Night's there to give us day, and God above
Made the whole universe for making love.
Just as a poet loves, just as the wise
Have not two faces, not two verities,
I have let beauty, paramount and proud,
Vanquish me always, treat me as it would;
I am ecstatic at a starry cloud,
A white swan on the water: then how could
I hide my joy at woman's pulchritude?

The birds far distant in the endless blue
Sing just one song, the song of Life. I pity you
If you have power; if you are loved, I envy you.

iv. *The Spoilsport*

They've skedaddled, beauties all,
Don't know where to hide themselves:
Dark and fair ones, big and small,
They were dancing near the bells.

One girl singing gave the rhythm.
Colourful, and quick, the lads
Gathered to be dancing with 'em,
Fixing flowers in their hats.

From the spring they came, the girls.
('I love Susan' cried the oak.)
They were dancing near the bells.
('I love Rose' replied the rock.)

Belfry. Bugbear, black and grim.
'Ugly creatures! Go!' he yelled.
Catch the crabby whiff of him!
Dainty feet were all dispelled.

All the dance has run away,
Blue eyes, dark eyes, every one,
Like a flock of birds that fly
From the chilly rain, all gone.

And the rout has hushed the higher
Tiers of trees, alarmed them too:
Girls who dance on earth inspire
Nests to chirrup in the blue.

'What's his trouble?' No-one sings.
Who can say? The man in black
Drove away the pretty things,
Drove their songs still further back.

‘What’s his trouble?’ ‘If I knew,
I would tell,’ Cock-Sparrow trills.
They shed tears like morning dew.
It’s Forget-me-not who tells:

‘Frankly, you do not excite,
Stimulate his appetite.
Butterflies love roses, but
Owls, unhappily, do not.’

v. *Ora, Ama: Pray and Love*

Along the banks the partridge trips and prances.

The clouds desire the moon to join their dances,
Surrounding her, to carry her away;
Come, little George: perhaps we two shall play
Down there, beneath the ancient willow-tree.

Night falls; men wash their limbs; out on the lea,
The reaper, scythe on shoulder, wipes his brow,
Returning to the farm. A twilight glow
Descends on figures laughing in the brook.

The parson shuts his breviary-book.
Too late to read: this remnant of the day
Prompts him, who may no longer love, to pray.
Love is dawn, prayer is evening, of the soul.

What is our love of woman, after all,
But prayer to the Lord? We bend our knee
To woman. You shall read this, finally,
When you’re a full-grown man. For now, you stare:

I speak to you as if my Charles were there.
The pink wing dies, the blue wing takes its chance.
Prayer vies with love in brazen arrogance;
Love vies with prayer in reverential dread.

The glade is bright, the day has hardly fled;
From fading skyline tolls the Angelus;
Great sky above us, gaunt and measureless!
Rampart of radiant darkness, untold wonder!

How shall we pass inside the house of thunder?
Young hearts repine, old heads are jittery;
Faced with the vague star-strewn immensity,
The thrum of dawn is like the sunset's tremor.

Prayer is the castle door and love the key.

vi. A Setting Free

This winter so harsh had left only one bird
In the cage where the songs of so many were heard.
There'd been a clean sweep in the oversized rookery:
A dear little blue-tit, once part of a family,
Was in there alone: all the rest were a memory.
With grain, rusks, and water in constant supply,
To observe dropping in the occasional fly
Was the whole of her joy: she was sullen and shy.
She had not one canary, not even a sparrow.
To be caged, bad enough; but to plough a lone furrow…
Poor bird, lonely sleeper, constrained at bright dawn
To plunge her beak under her feathers alone!
The sad little creature was frantic, not tame,
As she played with no partner the perch-spinning game;
She would make you believe she had just undertaken
To climb all the bars, in a sequence unbroken.
She'd fly about madly, then suddenly stay
Immobile and silent and hidden away.
Her gloomy puffed plumage, her dimness of eye,
Head under her wing with the sun in the sky,
Made clear her bereavement, her mourning, her longing
For the vanished, extinguished grand concert of singing.
This morning I went to her door, gave a push,
And stepped in.
There's a grotto, two poles and a bush,
So the prison is furnished; a fountain is spurting;
In winter we close it all up with a curtain.

✧

The bird saw the grim Brobdingnagian come:
She flew high, she flew low, she dived down in the gloom,
In the grip of unspeakable horror and panic:
The funk of the weak is both futile and manic.

She fluttered in front of my terrible hand;
I was up on a table, a good place to stand.
She, terrified, cowering, shrieking and shaking,
Collapsed in a corner, all mine for the taking.
When the behemoth lunges, what hope for the bantam?
Can you fight, when the monster, the lumbering phantom,
Has seized you, poor captive, wan, frail and defenceless?
She lay in my fingers, unmoving and senseless,
Eyes closed and beak open, the neck limply drooping,
The wings lying lifeless, not seeing nor cheeping;
I noticed her little heart trembling and leaping.

April is the dawn's twin brother:
Bright the one and red the other.
Ever laughing, ever wakeful
Seems this present month of April:
Everything, my lawn, my garden,
All these gardens, that horizon,
All in earth and sky rejoice:
Perfumed flowers, flaming stars,
Gullies gilt by festive furze,
Heavenly murmuring of bees;
Cress-beds' myosotis sips
Where the petalled water slips;
Grass-blades glint, harsh winter thaws;
Well-contented Nature has
Scent, song, and sunshine, freely giving.
Even empty space is loving.

I took the bird from the aviary
To the old wooden, ivy-girt balcony.

Renewal and sunlight and vibrancy!
I opened my hand and I said 'Go free'.
The bird headed out to the branchy fastness
And into spring's magnificent vastness;
And I watched it shrink in the sunny sky,
In the airy depths' rose-clarity;
And it flew away to the endless trees,
To the loves' and the nests' vague messages;
To seek white wings it was soaring careless,
Speeding to the branches to choose its palace,
To pools, and petals, where the new leaves rise,
Amazed to have entered into paradise.

So I stood in the sunshine's brilliant light
And I watched the poor bird in its freedom-flight.
I could see it was saved from its troubles below,
And I thought: *I was Death*, just a moment ago.

XI Stones Thrown at Jean

Brussels, Night of 27 May, 1871

I looked. Just by the corner, I could see
The one who threw the stone. So young to be
Almost a murderer. Almost a child!
Young man, a guardian angel must have smiled
On you: you could have killed this little love.
How quickly human hearts are emptied of
Warmth, when a priest misleads! Sly men can soon
Create a villain from a sad buffoon:
Donkeys come out as tigers. Wretched youth!
God barred your hand from this fine pious death.
You failed! Then fade, you sorry transient ghost:
My thoughts are with your mother. Go! Be lost.

Woman, no curse on you! Fair play from me:
Heaven beams mercy down. Who you may be,
And what your child, no matter: here's my blessing:
You're not to blame, you're not ripe for chastising.
In my sweet angel's name, I pardon him.
What came to earth in him? Elysium,
That has no weeping and no widows' veils,
But brings us heaven's stars and all its smiles!
He was your baby. At his birth, you thrilled
With joy and love. I dandled this dear child,
Jean, in my arms; he slumbered on your breast;
Under your roof he was the mystery guest:
He was an angel. Neither of you can
Be blamed, if he's become a ruffian.
The priest, himself a victim, racked by fear,
Is a deceiver, and we've let him rear
This child: he poured deceit into its mind,
Blinded its heart, for he himself is blind.

Sad pupil, cruel teacher, I forgive.
Evil has endless power to connive;
Protesting, I entreat the Shade above.
Madam, he knows not what he does, your son;
God's grain was in him, which the priest's undone.
Now here he is in dogma's deep dark wood,
At bigot's beck and call. The bad, the good,
He drinks it in; truth, falsehood, error, blood!
Strike! He obeys. Assassinate! He's here.
With such as person, can I be severe?
The height that salves the depth is Calvary.
Poor killers! On us martyrs you rely:
We, the assailed, the crucified, condone
The stupid nail, forgive the wretched stone:
We pardon, justly. Mother, since your son
Stones me, I bless you. There's my duty done.
And, woman, when you die, I hope you'll see
That son, beside your grave on bended knee,
Beating his breast, and falsehood's lamp expired
Within him. May his heart with truth be fired:
Less by the priest, more by the Lord inspired.

XII Jean Asleep – III

Jean sleeps: she lets her little soul take flight,
Poor exiled angel, to the infinite,
As into cherry-trees the sparrow flies.
She turns her face away from earth, and tries,
Before she has to drink our bitter broth,
To link up, from our shadows, with the skies.
Blessed tranquillity! Her hair, her breath;
Her colour, more transparent than a moth;
Slight gestures, and her calmness: all perfection!
Old Grandpa, like a country in subjection,
A happy slave, looks on admiringly.

She is the very smallest entity,
And yet the greatest, here below. A rare,
Vague smile is on her lips, from who knows where;
Her neck has little folds; you can inhale
Her essence, beautiful as asphodel.
Beside her is a huge-eyed doll, that's pressed,
From time to time, against the infant breast.
Picture this angel, see her if you will,
Mysterious, tremulous, invincible,
Slumbering; hope resplendent round her face,
Like stars; the foot exposed, the childish grace.
Oh! What a smile, inscrutable and deep,
She will retrieve for Grandpa from her sleep!
Untarnished shines the soul of a little child,
Like the empyrean, far above this world;
And it's a solace when we're old, to see
The dawn seek out our dusk, so willingly.

Don't wake her. She is sleeping, like a rose.
Sunk in her sleep, Jean muses to compose

What will out-heaven heaven. From lily to lily
Flitting, from dream to dream, she makes her honey.
The modest little soul works hard for hours:
Sips dreams, as bumble-bees go sipping flowers.

XIII Epic Story of the Lion

i. The Paladin

A lion had clamped its jaws around a child,
And carried it, unharmed, into the wild
Forest, where streams and birds'-nests are at home.
He'd seized it as one plucks a summer bloom,
Not really knowing why, nor even torn
The skin, through tender-heartedness or scorn;
Contempt, or loving-kindness, or defiance.
They're serious beasts, and generous, are lions.
The little prince was in a wretched plight:
Raw meat and grass his diet, weak with fright,
He cowered in the cave, half-perishing.
He was the offspring of the local king:
The boy was ten years old, with sweet bright eyes.
The king had just the one child otherwise,
A little baby girl of two; and since
He was quite old, his thoughts were with the prince,
The monster's prey. The country-folk were awed:
A lion more fearsome than their own liege lord!

A hero wandered in. They told the brave
Man what was up; he headed for the cave.

A hollow where the very sunshine paled,
And entered warily, was the cave that held
The giant beast, complete with rocky pillow.

The wood was in a swamp and in deep shadow,
Set with more branches than a cage has bars,
Dense in the Breton style with tangled briars.

This forest was "right worthy of its consul,"
(Virgil), with menhir sacred to Irmensul;
A jagged skyline ended and began it;
The cave was sculpted out of solid granite,
With mighty oaks for stormy retinue.
Caves detest cities, and to pay their due
May harbour some dark instrument of vengeance.
Respect the lion: the oaks intone the sentence.

A savage palace: and he stepped inside.
An air of rapine and of homicide
Hangs on the homes of tyrants: harrowing
Dark shadows. Yes, his host must be a king.
The master lacked for nothing, you could tell
From the bones; soft lighting from a central well,
Where thunderclaps had knocked a skylight through:
For conquerors a blurry haze will do,
An owl's idea of night, or, to an eagle,
The early dawn; more glare would not be regal.
Well, then, you had a tall and handsome room:
His Highness clearly slept on fronds of broom,
Without embroidered drapes; his drink, it's true,
Was blood, but then he took pure water too,
Quite simply, with no butler, bowl, or cup.
Enter the knight, well-armed from toe to top.

At once he looked around the lair.
One of the greatest lords was there
That you may see, with huge mane crowned:
The lion, in thought, his gaze profound.

For who can say if jungle beasts
Serve as exalted sylvan priests?
This was a lion that excelled,
Fearsome, big-clawed, not quickly quelled.
The knight moved forward up the room;
His step was loud, bright red his plume.
The beast was sunk in reveries;
The presence-chamber was at peace.
Old Theseus saw in gulfs of hell
Ixion, Sisyphus as well,
Naked by cold Avernus' wave:
No less forbidding was the cave.
The paladin, whom duty spurred
With "Right, get going," drew his sword.
Deliberate, and inspiring dread,
The lion slowly raised its head.

"Ho, grisly beast!" the warrior said:
"About your cave a child is hid.
Scanning your insalubrious lair
I do not see it anywhere.
I've come to fetch it: we shall be
Friends, if you give it up to me.
If not, I am myself a lion:
You'll perish, while the royal scion
Rests in his father's arms once more,
Far from your hot and reeking gore.
That's what the next pale dawn will see."

The lion said: "I disagree."

The knight advanced, and cried "On guard,
Sir!" brandishing his mighty sword.

You might suppose the lion roared:
But no, it smiled. (It almost purred.)
Don't make a lion smile. The duel
Between two champions was cruel,
As when the Indian jungles bleed:
The man with his extended blade
Against the beast with lengthened claws,
They grapple, and with slavering jaws
Most horribly the monster mauls
The man, one daring, one devouring,
Squeezing the flesh beneath the mail,
Savagely kneading iron and steel,
Crushing to bits cuirass and all:
Just as a child gets purple stains,
Dabbling in blackberries. The remains
Of crested helmet and brassards
One at a time the lion discards,
Until the bones are all laid bare.
And now the splendid cavalier
Is just a messy pulp inside
The thick cuirass. The lion devoured
The hero, went to sleep, and snored.

ii. The Hermit

A hermit came: approached the cave,
Rope round his belly, trembling, grave;
Clutching his cross he stepped inside.
There lay the knight, all pulpified.
The lion woke, yawned, opened wide
Its eyes, breathed deeply, and espied
Cord, woolly habit, man inside,
With big black hood; now satisfied,
Showed all its teeth and, full of state,
Spoke like a grinding rusty gate:
"Want something?" "Yes – my king." "What king?"
"Prince – " "Who?" "The child." "Call that a king?"
The hermit bowed. "O kingly one,
Why did you take the child?" "For fun:
Company for a rainy day."
"Release him." "No – he's mine." "Then say,
What's next? You'll eat him up?" "No way:
Not hungry." "Think of his grieving father."
"Men killed the lioness, my mother."
"His father's royal, like you." "Not true;
His voice is just a man's; if you
Hear mine, I'm the lion." "If he has
To lose his son?" "There's still the lass."
"Not much for a king." "My family
Is the wild crag, the greenwood tree,
The lightning overhead: these three."
"Have mercy on a royal highness!"
"There is no mercy – only sadness."
"What about paradise? I can
Get God's blank signature – *blanc-seign…*"
"Remove yourself, old holy man!"

The hermit went away.

iii. The Hunt and the Night

The lion, alone,
Filled with a wild beast's great oblivion,
Went back to sleep, and down came perfect night.
The menhir stood in moonbeams' ghostly light,
The pond became a shroud, the path a lie,
A dream the mystic dark locality:
The cave was still, the holy stars strode toward
The dawn; the moles and crickets in the sward
Lay safe; the lion's calm and rhythmic breath
Cheered the small creatures of the woods and heath.

Suddenly dogs were baying, there were shouts
Of men, the blare of brass: one of those routs
That sends the forest reeling drunkenly,
While nymphs in bed lie listening nervously:
The din of a tremendous hunt, that filled
The whole lake, shadow, mountain, forest, field,
Troubling that vast, untamed, and dreaming world.
The undergrowth was red with trumpery
Of flickering lights, mixed with the hue-and-cry;
The dogs were howling loud in search of prey,
And shadows danced about each open way.
A noble noise, whose triumph went before:
You would have said an army – which they were:
Soldiers the king had sent to storm the lair,
Rescue the prince, his only son and heir,
And bring the lion's blood-stained hide back home.
Out of what darkness does rebellion come?
From man, or beast? He knows, who said I AM:
All things are numbers, he is the total sum.

The soldiers were well-fed and fit and tanned,
Well-armed, with bows and hunting-spears to hand,

A proud and gallant captain in command.
Some had been fighting in a distant land,
And all were tested and courageous men.
The lion could hear the ill-intentioned din;
His baleful eye was open, but his head
Stayed on its rock, the pillow of his bed;
Only his great tail stirred and fidgeted.

Outside the spacious cave that gave no sound,
The tumult of the angry host, all round,
Was like a buzzing swarm of bees, that hound
A spider, or assault a netted bear:
The regiment of hunters simmered there,
Drawn up in battle order, well aware
The monster was gigantic, one who ate
A hero as a monkey eats a nut;
So lordly that his eye stared down the eagle;
Beyond the tiger's cunning, still more regal:
And so with formal siege they paid respect.
With hatchet-blows the tangled scrub was hacked;
The troops advanced, close-ordered; every tree
Tugged at their bowstrings, flexed their armoury.
They made no sound, because they hoped to hear
The lion tread dry leaves, if he was near.
The dogs – they know when silence is required –
Moved noiseless, open-jawed. The torches flared
In the green shrubs, and threw their elongated
Light on dense foliage, that the wind vibrated.
That's how a skilful hunt is organised.

Amid the boughs the cave was scrutinised,
A shapeless mass, deep in the ruck of trees,

Gaping, yet silent, with an air of peace,
Dreamily heedless of the martial throng.
Fire in a hearth makes smoke, the belfry's song
Swells from a town besieged; no glimmer here,
No echo; they observed, with nameless fear,
With hand on bow or pike, the eerie quiet
Of the tremendous cave; I don't know quite what
The dogs were muttering; we're less afraid
Of thunderclaps, than horrors in the shade.
Their task, to hunt the beast: they pressed ahead,
Scanning the fronds, in hope and yet in dread.
The scouts were looking sharp, each had his lantern:
They watched the yawning threshold of the cavern.
The trees were mute, and shuddered, looking on;
The march was orderly, a thousand strong;
Possibly more, keeping a steady pace...
Suddenly, look! The lion's fearsome face.

At once it all seemed hopeless. All the trees
Loomed bigger; strong men trembled at the knees.
In spite of that, the valiant bowmen drew,
And landed arrows on the lion, who
Was riddled with a squall of darts. The storm
Cannot shake Snowdon, or excite Cairngorm;
With like solemnity the lion frowned,
Shook nearly all the arrows to the ground.
Others in whom so many darts had stuck
Would probably have fled, not pushed their luck;
Blood streaked his flank; he stood there, face to face
With the army; they, not fancying the place,
Reckoned the monster might be god or demon.
The dogs, abashed, slank back behind the spearmen.

Silence. And then across the great outdoors
Of woods and sleeping marsh, the lion roars,
One of those black and monstrous roars, that scares
Us more than all that's holy; even dares
The Thunder, which half-wakes, and wants to know,
From highest heaven, Who thunders there below?

It was the end. They fled, and took the fray
With them, as when the wind blows mist away:
The army broke, and scattered to the four
Points of the compass, at that dreadful roar.
It took one moment: soldiers, chiefs and all
Thought themselves in some supernatural
Place where the mighty wrath of nature brews:
Destroyed and crawling, shaking in their shoes,
They hid, they vanished. "Mountains, forests, see!"
The monster cried aloud: "One lion free
Outweighs a thousand men in slavery."

As lava from volcanoes is the cry
Of beasts: one outburst soaring to the sky
Normally calms them. Lions may be more cool
Than gods. Beneath the old Olympians' rule,
"Suppose we did it," said the Herculeses,
"And strangled all the lions and lionesses?"
The lions said: "Let's shower them with mercies."
This lion, though, was sinister and sombre,
Black nightfall's child, the type whose rages linger,
Not quickly calmed, ferocious in his anger.
A beast at sundown is intent on sleeping:
Dogs are a nuisance if they come a-creeping;
This lion had been the butt of scouts and spies;
The generous woods had borne indignities.

He climbed the mountain, reared upon its crest,
Gave voice again; and, just as sowers cast
Seed far and wide, he spread his mighty roar
Down to the city for the king to hear:-

"King! You have shamefully assailed
Me, though I have not harmed your child;
I tell you this from far afield:
At dawn tomorrow I'll arrive
In your city, with the boy alive.
I invite as audience all your valets:
I shall eat your son inside your palace."

All night, the streams went running through the grass,
And the clouds strayed beneath the splendid stars.

How did the city greet the rising sun?

Dawn and the desert; people on the run,
Crying for mercy, terrified, soon gone,
While through the streets the mighty beast came on.

iv. The Dawn

The populace, aghast, was in the basements.
No use resisting. No-one on the battlements;
The gates yawned wide. They are so awe-inspiring,
These demigods, brute beasts of black despairing,
So grim and grand their cave, it is unwise,
Wrong to be there when they materialise.
The palace had a massive dome of gold,
To which the lion, slow and thoughtful, strolled,
Still bristling with the darts, which he ignored:
An oak-tree doesn't die because its hard
Husk has been battered. Archers he saw none:
The people quailed and left the beast alone.
The lion, calm, came on without a pause,
Holding the child unconscious in its jaws.

A little prince is human, as you know;
The sight made tears of blessed pity flow.
His body stagnant in the jaws of death,
The tender captive drooped in two beneath,
Pallid, but still unpunctured by the teeth.
Gagged by his prey, the lion couldn't roar,
Which for a monster is a fearsome bore:
His calm was furious and he glared the more.
No glint of missile at embrasured slit:
They may have feared an arrow's fatal hit,
Shakily aimed at the triumphant monster,
Might miss the lion and despatch the youngster.

Keeping his mountain promise, he rejected
The city as unwholesome, and directed
His steps towards the palace. Being sated
With dread, he hopefully anticipated

Finding a person to converse with. Lo,
The door like windblown reed swung to and fro.
He entered. Was there anybody? No.

Well, the king, shedding tears for his lost one, had fled
Into hiding. My goal is survival, he said:
For the people's well-being I'm needed, it's clear. –
Wild beasts are sincere, don't take kindly to fear,
And the lion, so large when a man is so small,
Felt the shame. In the dark of his leonine soul
He said: Wretch of a father! I'll feast on the son.
From the courtyard, through corridors, wandering on
Under fine golden ceilings, he came to the throne,
Which was empty; then chambers, red, yellow, and green,
Wide open, deserted, a desolate scene:
Through hall after hall went the terrible beast
In search of a suitable place for his feast.
He was hungry. He suddenly came to a stop.

In an alcove near the garden
Was a poor wee thing, forgotten
In the panic, rocked and cradled
By the big plain dream of childhood,
As the sun poured through the arbour,
Yes, the little girl was waking;
She was all alone, half-naked,
She, the king's own daughter, singing:
For a child sings on, no matter
Whether all around is silent.

A voice more soft than a lyre to be heard,
A little mouth with a great big smile,

A cradle, an angel in a tall toy-pile,
A crib for a Jesus, a nest for a bird,
Two eyes blue and deep, mysteriously bright,
Feet, arms, tummy, neck and legs all bare,
Covered to the navel by a vest of white,
A sunbeam in April, a sky-high star,
A lily-bud from heaven, to earth come down:
That was the infant, sweeter than dawn.

That's what the lion had seen.

He came through the door, things were shaking on the floor,
Where the toys were on the table, he reared his mighty head;
He had the sombre majesty of monster and of emperor,
The prey in his jaws made the horror even more.
And the child, she saw and she said:
O! my brother! My brother! O! my brother!
Standing pink in the light she was numinous and warm
And she gazed at the super-enormous form
Of the jungle giant with his eye defiant
To give Og, Gog and Magog a terrible fright
And to put them to flight.
Who knows what goes through those godlike heads?
She stood up tall by the narrow bed
And she wagged her finger at the monstrous head.
The lion by the cradle of silk and lace
Put her brother down before her face,
As a mother might do with her arms across,
And he said, "Here you are now. Don't be cross!"

XIV To Souls Flown Away

Those souls you recall
Return not, my heart,
Resolved, despite all,
To stay there apart.

Sphere rings upon sphere,
Sunbeams dance in blue air.
They were loved by us here;
Are they happier there?

When Saint-Leu was our home
We were under the bowers:
Overhead, the blue dome;
And how lovely the flowers!

We ran to the woods
Where red leaves would fall;
We hunted for beetles
By the old sunny wall:

We laughed the good laughter
That Eden once heard;
Repeated it after,
Word echoing word:

I told Mother Goose tales;
We were happy, dear God!
We cried out for joy
At the flight of a bird.

XV Praise to the Child: Laus Puero

i. Spoilt Children

Seeing the young have little dread of me,
A dreamer at their joy and jollity,
A rogue grandfather! – pious brows grow dark,
Frowning because I overstep the mark.
Infinite fatherhood has closed me in:
I'm just a good old smile, a helpless grin.
Dear loves! I am the grandpa unrepressed,
Forebear of little ones the dawn has blessed:
Sometimes I scan the moon abstractedly,
Claim it for them, perhaps a bit for me,
Grossly irrational as that may be.
I'm a weak king, not wanting to be feared
By my people, Jean and George. A grey old beard:
Grey force unfettered, raging to be good,
I let them leapfrog all the laws; I would
Urge on to crime their rose-pink polity;
I crave unhealthy popularity.
I'm old: chill night awaits me: it's my place
To love the dawn, the laughter and the grace;
But for the little ones, unstained by crimes,
I ask you if their grandpapa sometimes
Should play the anarchist, might point the way,
As if to dark adventure, might betray
The solemn cupboard where the jam is stored!
Yes, I have perpetrated, I have dared
– Good women of the household, shed your tears! –
The rape and pillage of those sacred jars.
Disgracefully, for them I climb on chairs!
If in some corner I see strawberries
Reserved for our dessert, I rhapsodize:

'Dear little greedy birds of paradise,
All this is yours. See the poor children there,
Huddled beneath our window? One's a bare
Month old. They're hungry! Ask them up, and share.'

Off with the mask! Those maxims are mistakes,
Which ban the mighty eagles from the peaks,
Love from the smooth breast, pleasure from the child.
We're dreary, tiresome, stuffy. How I've smiled,
Laughed, when we let our adult fury grow
If a child steals an apple, yet allow
Kings to swear perjured oaths. Good yeoman, please,
Defend your rights, not just your apple-trees!
Dishonour's tide floods like the rising seas,
And, shamefully, the bourgeois vote agrees;
Conmen are bishops, fraudsters own the banks;
A gambler lays a wager over France:
Like one who moves a pawn across a board,
He sits impassive, sombre, unperturbed;
Plays the grim game of an adventurer:
Tails he's a convict, heads an emperor!
And none prevents, and fury there is none,
As treason's crude debauch ascends the throne!
So to the cradles I retire, and flee
To the sweet dawn: for I would rather see
This swarm of innocents, these merry elves,
Swayed by mere whimsy to amuse themselves,
Than crowds who wallow and condone the crime
With flags and feasting. Paris, I've no time
For all your vicious, low-imperial den.
Better spoilt children, than corrupt old men!

ii. The Syllabus

You're eating your oranges in a nervous way,
My little tremulous angels. I think today
I quite frighten you;
But why? You can count on my kindness, Jean, dear child,
For it is a grandfather's business to be mild,
Heaven's to be blue.

Don't be frightened. Yes, I may seem to be cross, I scold,
But it isn't at you. Sadly, in this hard world
The priest loathes and lies:
And even deep in our green retreat, I hear
The daily round of garbage, the hubbub of mere
Imbecilities.

The priesthood casts a shadow. Out in the plain,
There's sunshine: I want it. Come along, George and Jean,
Brother, sister, both.
The sun's on the lake, on the thatch the dawn is bright,
Ascending to God from everything, there is light;
Blackness, from the cloth.

I love one smallness, I can't abide the other:
I abominate theirs, I adore your wittering chatter.
When you speak, my dears,
I lean down to garner the words of a soul that's pure
And I seem to be gazing through some vague aperture
In the heaven of stars.

For only a day ago, my sweet-talking strangers,
You held conversations with stars, and with the angels;
You have no wrong-doing.
You bring to my scowling thundercloud a gleam,
A ray of the unknown morning: you have come
From where I am going.

What you say comes out of the firmament austere:
Something beyond the human and earthly sphere
Is in your young eyes;
And your voice, which will not wound and will not blame
Nor bite, is part of a mighty wedding-hymn,
The woods' mysteries.

I like your gentle murmurs: I sense the ideal:
It pleases me. Now I may appear to loll
In the forest groves;
Yet God knows well, that when water finds the top
Of the rocks, I hark to its falling, drop by drop,
Through the far cool caves.

What we call death and what we call life elide,
Speak in one tongue to the soul unsatisfied,
For below we starve;
But to dream is to soar in the high celestial realm,
And to comprehend: and the nests all say the same
As the chilly grave.

The priests go crying: Anathema! Curse on curse!
Nature answers, I love you! in all the universe.
Come, children: there's light
Shining all around us, and everywhere bursts with joy;
The infinite swells with blue, it's the dawn of day;
Loving souls take flight.

Against these black-clad pygmies I've spoken loud;
But the flowers are fragrant now, so don't be cowed,
And the woods are wild:
Spring's here, the glorious festival. Now and again
I've given a fright to certain stunted men,
But not to a child.

iii. Envelope of Money that Jean Collected for Charity

My friends, who wants joy?
We all of us do;
Then let us be giving
To the poor on their knees,
Under cover of evening.

As he weeps in the ways,
Or, wretchedly naked,
Lies starved, stricken, shaking,
The poor man assays
The heart that is human.

To reject him is sadness,
To aid him is gladness.
This humble old man
With chattering teeth,
This street-corner ghost,

Sick, dragging his feet,
Can bring our vexed souls
Starry joy that comes down
From paradise caverns.

Are you downcast? You are.
Then give, give again.
For the pittance of gold
Or of silver you throw,

You, rich and uncaring,
Who now and then mock
The poor in their hovels,
God gives you the light
That can fill up your heart!

For your spangle of yellow
Or white, filthy penny,
So precious to you,
God offers you back,
In the hand stretched for alms,
A star of his heaven.

iv. On the So-called Law of Freedom in Education

Priests, you conspire to save us, with the aid
Of shadows; you defy the light with shade,
Your murky remedy.
You who would set man free, you leave him fettered:
You have found out a virtue, which is hatred,
And love's the felony.

You are the mob attacking the sublime:
The mighty mind of Man aspires to climb
To the truth's topmost storey.
Alas, his brow resurgent in the gloom
Draws to its radiance the dismal swarm
Of dogmas roused to fury.

The lion roars and growls and tries to kill,
In vain; the insect strives, the vermin still
Presumes, inveterate;
The loathsome whirling horde incurs our scorn;
We let you rail: we watch great Babylon
Assailed by Lilliput.

Do we see Nineveh the hundred-towered
Reduced by grubs, by woodlice overpowered?
Or Thebes the hundred-gated?
Do we observe Olympus, Pelion, Pindus,
The Himalayan peaks beyond the Indus,
By vulture-flights prostrated?

Voltaire and Diderot, twin fortresses,
Defy your flailing wings; and Horace's
Dear Plato stands unbowed;
Old Dante in his fastnesses, adorning
The skies with gold, opens like gates of morning,
That wake the peaks from cloud.

That granite mountain-rock, the Pyramid,
Erect in Egypt, sandstorm-buffeted,
By djinns and demons haunted,
Crude hieroglyphic, has no inkling that
It's grazed by talons of the flitting bat,
By filthy dung affronted.

Bite as you may, the future cannot die.
Divine and sure the darts of morning fly;
We see, and shall prevail!
For truth kills error; nights must yield to days;
Dawn has a quiverful of shining rays:
No fear that it should fail.

And so your shame fills heaven's endlessness!
You live; yet the Ideal has no less
Bright morning in her eyes.
Benign reality forgives the lie;
And I myself shall be consoled, as I
Dream under sacred skies,

So long as Jean shall be my earthly guide,
And I shall journey, and the Lord provide
(Pure mystery divine!)
All the Ideal that can be possible:
Two joys: a great star in my tranquil soul,
A little hand in mine.

v. Penniless Children

Watch this little one with care,
Filled with God, and great in worth;
Babes, before they come to birth,
Shine above in azure air.

God in bounty gives us this:
They are sent to us on earth,
All his wisdom in their mirth,
All his mercy in their kiss.

We are warmed in their sweet light;
They are cold, and heaven shivers;
They are hungry, Eden suffers;
Happiness is theirs by right.

Men have angels in their power:
Every innocent unfed
Puts on trial the evildoer.
Thunder's rage shall wake the dead:

God, who sent these pretty things
To our den of sleep and shadows,
Sent them down to us with wings,
Finds them wearing rags and tatters!

vi. In the Fields

With tenderness I look down on the waters and woods,
A dreamer, a grandfather too of the flowers and birds:
I have for things that holy and deep compassion.
I stop the children mistreating roses. "Don't frighten
The plants and animals: laugh but don't alarm,"
That's what I tell them. "Play but do no harm."
Jean and George, with wondering eyes and brows serene,
Go beaming about the splendid flowery scene;
I roam, and I don't disturb, all this paradise;
I hear them sing, and I think, and I recognise
That they pay no heed in their charming escapades,
They ignore the sombre sound of the turning pages
Of the cryptic book where is written the fateful word.
They are far from the priest, they are very near Our Lord.

vii. Again the Immaculate Conception

Wait. There's a little girl I see,
A stranger, singing radiantly.
Here's laughter, daylight, beauty, sky:
I cannot just pass coldly by:
She's dawn itself! – She's not yet three.
Perhaps she should be more discreet,
But doesn't know it: which is sweet.
No bishop's yellowed pompous phiz
Can be as heavenly as this.
Kids' babble is my bibliothèque:
I scan their comments like a book:
The meaning's great, at times severe,
Profound; and so I bend to hear
This angel-chatter that assuages
And reassures, and calms my rages,
Dispels that bilious sombre shadow,
Basilio's slanderous sombrero,
And helps me laugh at foes' bravado.
This child's a heart, a hideaway,
A party on a festal day;
God gives her every breath and word,
From meadow bud, from woodland bird.
My Jean could be her twin. Last year
She used to drag a cart, like her,
Emptied it, filled it, laughed and ran.
Every child has one; every man
Likewise! And so, child, pull your cart!
Have fun, and wait for life to start.

Praise be! How children grant me peace!
Sweet thing, your hands – look, what a mess!
Put on your stockings, ma'moiselle!
Barefoot, mud-spattered, beautiful;

Cart broken! She's like us, *ma foi*:
Any old thing can be a car.
Triumphal cars for child and man:
Like us, they have their silly fun,
Make laws that bind and beat them down:
They haul their rattle, we our sovereign:
Only, we wallow, they stay pristine.
Look, who comes here? A smaller one:
Toddler – her sister. Great big hat:
A smile, oh! trembling! delicate:
A masterpiece. Show off your foot!
She points her toe and sings. Divine!...
To think (does Veuillot speak in vain?)
They flaunt the old, the *primal stain*!
They are "*The Fall*". Patouillet's phrase
"Adam's vile poison" merits praise.
Eve *smirched the sky*! The young are *sins*,
Loathsome, though sweet as frankincense.
Their beauty adds to the offence,
Their grace compounds our penitence,
They soil Mamma with radiance.
Dawn loves them; flowers bestow their scents:
Disgrace, got up as innocence!
Trublet denounced, in these bright eyes,
The demon's sinister disguise:
It's evil, hellish, comes from the abyss!
Right. Let me give them cakes, these felonies.

viii. Jean, Wife and Mother

To see the Jean of Jean! O what a dream is there!
The holy shadows hide a virgin heaven where
A sun – who knows what sun! – delights who knows what eyes.
The souls to come are cradled there in brilliant skies;
God guards them, till their life shall start. The souls await,
Between the two horizons, their uncertain fate:
One lies before, one after they come here to live:
One lies beyond the cradle, one beyond the grave.

I think about that sphere we cannot know:
There in pale swarms, confused but joyful, go,
The thronging floods of souls, eyes opened wide:
I look at angel Jean with God inside,
And the young lads at play beneath my window:
Youth light of heart, that age untouched by sorrow,
Loves in the embryo, bridegrooms in the bud:
I ponder. Jean goes running in and out,
Pulls her cart, holds her trowel, gives a shout,
Delves in my papers, digs the grass; she skips,
Chattering, fills the house with light; she weeps,
Her tears are dew, a sunbeam is her laughter;
I lob my thoughts ahead, two decades after,
A witness of some future happening,
As when a stone goes hurtling from a sling.

A sunrise is not made to be alone.
My soul's the forebear of that childish one:
My heart descends to hers, and thoughtfully
Involves itself in her young destiny.

One day, some morning, fresh and dazzling bright,
Shall wed that daybreak still adorned with stars;
Some soul, that now is roaming secretly
Where we sense all the future rests in God,

Shall seize the moment to be born on earth,
Out of a kiss that these two dawns exchanged.
You tender wood-bird shrilling in your nest,
A voice cast wide amid the waving trees,
Singing the song of spring – you turtle-dove,
Warbler or titmouse, dreamlike fugitive
That wings from branch to branch, soft undertone
Folded in scented meadows: I am here,
I listen, I am full of dreams. Love well,
You who shall live! Chaste god of marriage! Nature!
Jean shall be on the verge of her adventure,
In her my fate increases, and shall pause;
She'll be the mother, young and earnest-browed,
The guardian of a sunrise that must live,
Dutiful wife, devoted nurturer,
Soft heart severe; and it shall be her turn
To stoop in anxious love, diaphanous
And heavenly, above the fragile crib.
Bright dreams! My Jean shall contemplate her Jean,
Console her weeping and attend her cries,
And join her hands in prayer. She shall feel
Her life all mixed with this young life; for her
She'll dread the cold, the wind, fear everything
And nothing. Ah, how frail the peach-tree's flower!
Soon as the dear sweet angel-child can walk,
She'll take her to the Tuileries to play;
Children, all running where the branches bloom,
Mingling man's April with God's greater one.
More women, happy under one blue sky,
Shall be there too, like Jean, and take delight
In this unfolding, blossoming of souls;
Each pretty face attentive to the young,
These mothers, sisters before God, shall smile
As all these countless roses dazzle them.

I shall be just an eye, set deep in shade.

ix. Be Giants

What can I do? I'm in the child's control;
I end up loving innocence, that's all.
All men are lead and brass, the child is gold:
I dote on Hector's boy: himself, I scold.
Has our own Troy gained benefit from you?
My skies are cloudless, but they thunder too.
Kindness and fury are my ebb and flow:
Both are unlimited, whether I show
A smiling face, or strike up cold and harsh:
I feel my soul's profound, and set with stars;
My heart is vast: rights of the powerless,
The strong support we owe the penniless,
Love of the child: no limits are in place;
If that's a sickness, I'm a hopeless case.
Winging to man from heaven goes the ray
Of shining light. It never stops halfway!
Economy of truth, I never learned:
Let smiles be frank, let stars be unadorned.
I'm old, and, sad or happy – passably –
More or less father of the century:
I'll grant your wish, extreme as it may be,
A useful grandpa, giving willingly
A criticism, or a eulogy.
I was a winner once. I needed air:
The winners were so ruthless, so unfair:
I fled. A crag, a barren strand, conferred
A welcome. Death came up to have a word:
Exile, I greet you, Sir! And someone smiled,
Someone who looms and dreams, deep down concealed:
My conscience: and I loved just any child,
Mysterious heaven!.. I am far less worth:
A child is love, a child is all good faith.
Only one being on our sombre earth

Is small, yet great, not knowing jealousy:
The child.
                    – Which makes these sparrows dear to me.

But I see heroes in these myrmidons:
France, I await their dutiful response.
Soon as our sons arc grown, I smile no more:
I call on them to wage a mighty war
On scaffolds, sceptres, towers, thrones, the sword.
Soft on the young, on fathers I am hard.
Give me grown men! Our mother, France, is seized,
Gripped by her hair: they drag her by her feet
All round the vandal camps; the feudal beast,
Deformity reborn, insults the light,
Two snarling heads that quarrel, fight and bite:
Rome and Berlin. The greatest of affronts,
It breaks my heart, is our poor shrunken France:
I tell young shavers: Old as Alexander?
Don't be a blockhead! be a great commander!
Daybreak reproaches me, there's only gloom,
Only eclipse: I'm envious of the tomb.
Grieving, I conjure up our forebears' deeds:
Great cliffs assaulted by our surging floods,
Crumbling away before the Marseillaise;
The gates of night, dragons and hydra-heads:
All that, our valiant soldiers set ablaze!
I see the lightning flashing on their flags,
Recall the savage joy of their attacks:
They twisted Europe in their brazen fists,
Those soldiers of the Rhine, the Nile, the Argonne,
Fighters, avengers. Do as they have done!
Angels are sweet; but I'm a no-holds-barred
Forebear: I want archangels, with the sword!

Ancestral scold, or grandpapa mild-mannered,
I love great glory: we should wallow in it,
When it is sacred to our country's cause.
I don't want Rheims or Paris or Toulouse
Lumped with extinct Pompeii; I don't see
Why souls should crawl and cower wretchedly;
Or why we shouldn't match the audacity,
The toil, the hopes, the deaths of those who fought
At Ulm, the Pyramids, and Jena. What?
Have heroes fathered shirkers? No! – Young men,
Your blood is rich: and they were valiant, when
They stunned the bad old world. There's still a place
To be a people, not a populace:
You shall be giants too. There are no reasons
Why I should not desire the same horizons,
Same nations with a song again unfettered,
Same feudal pomp destroyed, same prisons shattered,
Same greatness gilding, uninhibited,
Our living children as our forebears dead!

XVI Two Songs

i. Grandfather's Song

Dance, little daughters,
  In a ring.
Seeing your sweetness,
  Woods shall sing.

Dance, little queen-bees,
  In a ring.
Lovers in ash-groves
  Dallying.

Dance, little dreamers,
  In a ring.
Books in the schoolrooms
  Muttering.

Dance, little beauties,
  In a ring.
Birds with their wing-beats
  Welcoming.

Dance, little fairies,
  In a ring.
Cornflower headbands
  Shimmering.

Dance, little ladies,
  In a ring.
Gentlemen's words come
  Flattering.

ii. Ancestor's Song

Let's speak of our forebears under the greenwood tree.
Let's speak of our fathers, boys! They broke their chains,
They conquered; and now their armour has rusted away!
Like water cascading down from a sodden sponge,
From their soul in the shadowy depths the lightning rained,
As if they were flecked with brimstone, in thunder plunged.
Thrum, you scholars,
Swords on bucklers!

They dreaded the dismal wine and the dance-drunk jades:
They were affronted, these sons of Brennus the Gaul,
To see kings passing proud under colonnades,
For the kings' processions were endless promenades
Of priests and soldiers and soft breasts bared to all,
Of incantations and censers and severed heads.
Thrum, you scholars,
Swords on bucklers!

They craved, they conjured, they wrought deliverance.
They were the Titans, we are the crawling worms.
They knew that Gaul would be the mother of France.
A mountain is promised the sunshine: it happily dreams,
Nor is it disappointed when daylight dawns.
Thrum, you scholars,
Swords on bucklers!

The Princes fashioned a League. It was no great matter,
Perhaps, and nor did they care if their chief cried Haste!
Yet they roared, and came at a run: and the kings were chased
From the field, and took to their heels, just as lute-songs scatter
At once on the winds, for the lack of a minstrel's taste.
Thrum, you scholars,
Swords on bucklers!

They fought with the deeps, they toppled the crowns of crime,
Smashed the black altars, led crooked gods in chains!
As I brood above the void in my waning-time,
I declare them great. For one thing is more sublime
Than Ocean with its vertiginous hurricanes:
Man the hero, man in the grandeur of war's refrains!
Thrum, you scholars,
Swords on bucklers!

We are their sons! yet we blew out the light they lit.
Proud forebears! they sent the false priest empty away.
They quenched the fires of the wretched *auto da fe*;
And many great spirits that Satan unjustly set
To suffer (God knows!) were saved by their aid from the pit.
Thrum, you scholars,
Swords on bucklers!

Lift up your eyes! See that perfect summit of glory:
They were there; see that peak of honour and self-respect:
They were there. Look now at that lofty promontory
Called Liberty: they died free with their heads erect.
Licence, debauchery, these are false delights;
The time will return, to climb those arduous heights.
Thrum, you warriors,
Swords on bucklers!

XVII Jean Asleep – IV

A bird sings; I'm in reveries, and she
Is sleeping, in the pink, beneath a tree
In blossom. Like a halcyon's nest, her cradle
Stirs; she ignores the gliding sun and shadow
Above her closed eyes. She is very small,
Delectable, and supernatural.
How beautiful is children's innocence!
I muse, she dreams; and on her brow descends
A swarm of visions, interlaced, serene:
Women from heaven, every one a queen
To look at; angels, friendly-looking lions;
Small heroes shielding poor and virtuous giants;
Splendour of flowers in the woods, and trophies
Of heavenly trees, full of the glow of fairies;
A demi-paradise, set on a cloud:
All this is showered on the sleeping child.
A dreamland palace is the baby's cradle,
On which God pours confections, all delightful;
Hence their fresh smile and deep tranquillity.
Some will say, later: 'God, you cheated me.'
'No!' God replies, from very depths of gloom;
'Heaven is your dream; I gave you heaven's shade.
But heaven shall be yours, not long delayed:
Another cradle waits for you: the tomb.'

That's what I dream. It's springtime. Bird, give song!

XVIII What They Will Read Later On

i. *Our Country*

France, your sad fate affronts and angers me.
I've said it, and will say it constantly.
My soul cries out against the infamy
Of one who hurts my mother: though he be
Concealed, I hate him! and I long to see
Him pay, on earth or in eternity.
Caesar I flay; I shake the vaults of doom,
Question the shadow, delve in miry gloom.
The brigand Emperor, the bandit Chance,
Both rouse my rage. Criminal Circumstance,
Benighted Fate! I sob, and wail, and curse
The wretched joker, Destiny, in verse.
The night, the abyss, dire happenings, black sky,
I call them all to order: I defy
Sinister interests that nullify
True rights by hoodwink and by trickery.
They have no right to bar the road of Reason.
I rail against reverses born of treason.
Honour and glory ambushed! I affirm
It's God himself who stumbles. Facts that squirm
And skulk, I cross-examine: victory,
Winter, the darkness, all their treachery;
I tell these dingy transients of the abyss:
'I see you at your crime: take note of this:
We are not kneeling: we are men, aware
And thinking beings: you should have a care:
This is no way to carry on with France.
Though plunged in deepest hardship and mischance,
Even entombed, a star shines on her brow.'
How will they answer me? I'd like to know.
I am persistent, I can look askance,

Disconcert Fate with disapproving glance:
We must account to heaven, rest assured.
When progress falters, when it seems the Lord
Grows smaller, shrinking in the savage gloom,
When Man's a skiff with Satan at the helm,
Clearly the human soul is locked in jail:
Something above us isn't right at all.

That's why I demand that the shadows reply.
I'm not one whose courage will turn tail and fly,
Who looks at the triumph of villain and lout,
Loses trust in his rights, is in funk and in doubt.
No, I brush down my sandal and lengthen my stride:
My soul has no record of turning aside.
I don't take it hard if the surge and retreat
Of our destiny brings us another defeat.
Lost battles remind me of battles victorious;
My memory's stubborn, invincibly glorious.
There's life in the folds of our old winding-sheets:
When I read 'Waterloo', I pronounce 'Austerlitz'!
If I file by the grave, if I mourn for the dead,
My funeral garb puts more height on my head.
But it isn't enough: I demand they be honest
Up there in the deep and mysterious forest –
I'd watch the Fates work – for whatever they do,
It's we who must suffer, right here, me and you.
I face down the chasm: I dare, for I know
We must hold to account the grim Shadows below.
Why are these taken from us, I'm eager to know,
Our cities, our army, our practical powers?
Why the chopping and cheating, the filching what's ours?
We're a vast, loving people, a splendour aglow!
What's the root of our troubles? I just want to know,
To see right to the core of our pitiful fate,
To the corners where clarity can't penetrate...

Why the warm South by the cold North done in?
Why living Paris crushed by dead Berlin?
Angels in chains, a barebones throned; O France!
I shall indict our battles, wars, affronts,
And sorrows; I shall have these thieves turn out
Their pockets; for it is a prophet's right
To judge events; nor should the moral law
Be blown about by force superior.
Events can be malignant: they may err.
A warning to the void: I'm losing patience;
And there you find the grandeur of our Conscience:
Sad and alone, supported by no more
Than innocence, the weak man's plea at law,
The cradle and the reed; she still by Justice,
(One word!) arrives in heaven. At the solstice,
She may correct a shooting-star, that strays;
She calls on God, to help the human race;
She is the pure white Truth, that cannot die;
Might is not Might, in her vicinity;
Laws unrevealed are to her cause inclined;
Her strength and beauty (priest, bear this in mind!)
Stem from rejecting that an outrage can
Be planned and purposed by a righteous man;
Armed but with naked truth, when lightning lands
Unjustly on this earth, when there descends
Another stroke out of the mystery,
Dark groping menace to humanity:
If she would climb to question it on high,
In that great cloud of darkness we have held
In reverence: then, for all that she is mild,
Thunder itself would stutter and be stilled.

ii. Perseverance

Let's see it through. When man has grasped the key,
Doors are soon opened. Tired of evil, she
Herself, the Night, may open wide her eyes,
Calling for somebody who clarifies.

Problems are there to show us remedies.

The darkness growls at us, draws back aghast.
Consider the great thinkers of the past,
Heroes and giants fired by one same soul,
Cut off by death from their exalted toil:
They pass with starry brows and dusty feet.
Salute their unyoked harness and their sweat,
And march! For we must also run our stage,
March with the footfall of a future age.
Forward! Succeed them in the path they made!
Leave all the past in ever-thickening shade,
Leave it behind us, dwindling far away,
Leave out of sight the crimes of yesterday.
Precursors lit these hazes bright and clear:
Plato stood there, Luther ascended here;
See the great beacons of great forerunners:
The murk is filled with torchlight of the seers.
Here is the precipice where Pascal stood:
'Chasm' he cried! ...I tread where Rousseau trod;
Here too, enlightened, consummate, aware,
Set free from earth, to heaven soared Voltaire.
'I see!' he cried – a dazzled prophet's cry.
Join in their battle! Fight with head held high!
Forward! Each step unveils another field:
The times are new, new laws shall be revealed:
The heart is open and the spirit sound;
And we have proud new doctrines to propound.

✧

Live, march, believe! Be tranquil, everyone.
– But deathly civil strife, long years of pain,
Enmities, tears, the disinherited,
The hurt, the banished, all who mourn their dead,
Endemic hatred, in our hearts piled high –
Won't it explode, a vast incendiary?
Anger spreads wider, rampant fury rears,
The skies are black – but see, the weather clears!
What's fury? What is anger worth? Who cares?
Vengeance will marvel at the fruit it bears!
God's task is to transform us in our night,
Abort the thunderbolt, induct the light.

God takes the hatred in our hearts, consumes it all away;
He throws himself upon us from his fastnesses of day,
    And severs from our soul all things but love;
He probes with conscience' metal rod our dreams and meditations,
Explores our breasts and bowels below, we like to call them passions,
He steals our evil instincts and he strips out all that soils,
    All causes of our torment he'll remove.
And when he's made us perfect, like the blessed sky above,
    All good and pure, he flies off heavenward;
And greater for his coming down, for hate has turned to love,
    The soul gives thanks, and wants to know,
    Who gripped me in his talons so?
And thinks it is an eagle, and perceives it is the Lord.

iii. *Progress*

Forward march, humanity!
People, change your region.
Grub, become an entity,
Flock, become a legion.
Eagle, speed to daybreak: see,
Only night-owls cannot be
With the dawn as it ascends.
In the sun we may divine
God; for its rays have soul divine,
And soul human, at their ends.

From one to other see it fly;
It is thought and clarity,
Messenger of earth and sky,
Freedom below and flame on high;
Formed Horace's and Dante's mind
And gilds the rose hung on the wind,
The chaos of our wandering;
And with one emerald touches in
The humming-bird's exiguous wing
And the dragon's scaly skin.

Take the paths of shining flares,
Take the starlit thoroughfares,
Souls who glean and minds who sow,
Onward, onward, onward go!
Sorry slaves of yesterday,
From the stews of shame, away!
Valiantly march and climb!
Climb to glory, dusky throng:
As you quit the sordid slime,
Let this be your triumph-song.

Sail the seas, and sweep away
All the past in ocean spray;
Smash the gallows; at your prow,
Burn the hangman's noose, with tow.
Crush in their ooze the beasts of old;
Scale the mountain-tops, be bold:
Be as sun-gods are, for pure
Is the sword of righteous war.
Run your course! For you are shod,
At your heel, in hydra's blood.

iv. Fraternity

I dream of fairness and of truth, deep down,
Love longing, hope shining, faith founding;
The people enlightened, not chastised.
I dream of sweetness, kindness, and compassion,
And a great mercy. So, I am alone.

Man's ancient cruelty is self-excusing.
A priest, a judge, assumes he has the right
To any pleasant action of his choosing:
He wears his robe and lays his conscience by.
That's how we deal with heaven's equity:
Strip off what's awkward, clothe it as we please;
Bilk children, women, and the weak, defease
Their proper rights, sell short, give less for more,
Replace God's justice with cheap human law.
Hence the Sun-Kings, the men as great as God,
The cobblestones awash with streams of blood;
Hence Cumberland, Judge Jeffreys, Colonel Pride,
Wide lands distraught and cities terrified,
Stonings, atrocities, and black cortèges,
And furrowed foreheads of affronted sages.

Comes Jesus. Who says 'He must die'?
The man of God. Sharp agony!
Always, whatever we imagine,
The Furies batten on religion.
Megæra used to be a Christian;
Tisiphonê the bloodstained sister
Sang antiphons for the Inquisitor:
Her voice still echoes in the cloister.

The 'dragonnades'! They howled again
For massacre, through glade and glen:
Those demons spurred Letellier's son
To slaughter: Bossuet drove him on.

If God himself should intercede,
Man's ancient madness won't recede,
Shrink backward from the bright horizon:
On the clean wind it sprays its poison,
Fouls with its rage the love-song's fabric,
Withdraws at night, resumes at daybreak.
Progress, though fine, wise, true, and just,
Lives with the monster, as it must.
Consider how the tyrant falls:
The day that Cromwell strikes down Charles,
Cromwell remains, a tyrant still.
This spectral plague, dawn can't dispel!
The villain dies, vile ways persist.
Good sense, stern smiling exorcist,
Attacks the vampire, doesn't win:
Cruelty's in our hearts, dug in,
Grips sires and sons and never leaves,
Like a dark grandam in the eaves.
Then, our old continent conceives:
The ideal's born! The people rise,
Jubilant; in one day, July's
Thrown all the Bastilles on the wind,
And Liberty astounds the mind.
Freedom! On mountains and on oceans
Your daughters rear, the revolutions,
Winning the battle of the titans;
The whole world sees the past in flight,
Vanished and void; ghost, shade, and night.
Backlash. Barbarity and Error

Lose Torquemada, gain the Terror.
They do not find this sunrise onerous!
Mankind's great hive, aroused and sonorous,
Heads for the blue and shining hours,
Makes honeys various as the flowers,
Labours and sings. Old hateful Cain,
Seeing our Eden rise again,
Stuck in his old ways to the last,
Chains rosy dawn to rotting past:
Old Hatred keeps his ancient pit,
And, if his chain's not up to it,
Replaces the Decree of Nantes
With revolutionary rant.
So Satan with his gang accursed
Laughs, as our paradise is lost.
My heart, my heart, we've not been raving:
Man should be good, and great, and giving,
And merciful, merciful, evermore!
Shout mercy, till your throat is sore.

It isn't lunatic to wish the swan
More sunrise, or the children's night-time gone;
It isn't wrong or idle, I believe,
To groan for the oppressed, or bid us Love.
It isn't false or fanciful to hold
That man's not born black-hearted, sinful-souled;
There's good concealed in evil, and in fact
The fault's not often his, who did the act.
Man is to evil as the glass to air:
Gauges the cold, a true barometer,
Adds nothing: he may rise or may descend;
Blame it on that dark passer-by, the wind.
Man's a mere flag some evil tower displays:
He feels each breath that shudders, slithers, plays

And floats and blows. He should by rights be pardoned,
A living rag, hauled up aloft, abandoned.
Grant pardon, man to man, brother to brother!
In tempest and abyss, pardon each other,
Grant pardon! Brave hearts bleed, the years are brief:
Then grant to one another this relief!
If I myself slip up, transgress, and fall,
It is the darkness that's responsible:
Cold comes from winter, error comes from night;
Forgiveness, love, compassion are my right.

One day I saw passing a woman unknown.
This woman it seemed from the clouds had come down;
On her back were two wings, and her lips were half open,
And dripping with honey; her eyes spoke of heaven.
To the lost without number who wearily stray
In the shadow, she seemed to be pointing the way,
And saying: One sometimes goes wrong by mischance.
The whole human race felt the grace of her glance:
She was radiant and sweet, and as if on a string
She led well-behaved monsters, each kissing her wing:
There were tigers repentant and lions in grace,
Nimrod pardoned, and Nero with tears on his face.
She was sometimes so good that I found her absurd.
Well, I fell on my knees, never saying a word;
I thought that I knew her, and dumbly adored.
But, faced with an angel, our privacy's gone:
She read all my thoughts, and said: "Need I let on?
You think I am Mercy. I'm Justice, my son."

v. The Soul Pursuing Truth

1

I'll speed in the sombre chariots
Of vision and of dream:
Into the pale shadow-city
I'll pass like a sunbeam.
I'll hear their bleary cries;
In the clouds I shall seem
The wild man of the air:
Beneath my feet the sheer
Drop, my gaze wondrous, more
Than lightning and meteor.

I'll return to my abode
In the black world limitless,
Hurl earth into infinity
And time into eternity;
I'll kick away our misery.
In my talons I shall seize
The truth. I'll be transfigured:
Hardly a trace there'll be
Of human luminosity
Astir in my sacred eye.

For I'll be no more a man:
I'll be the dazzled spirit,
The tomb shall tell me its name,
The riddle shall not deny me.
What if the shadows are fearsome,
I shall spread my arms as awesome
As Thales in antiquity,
Elias in Gethsemane,
In the tremendous ecstasy
Of nothing and infinity.

I'll interrogate the gulf
On the universal secret,
The volcano, urn of sulphur,
And the ocean, urn of salt:
What they know in their fastness,
What their agonies lave,
I'll sound it out; and I'll go
Forward, until in the shadows
I touch with wings of the grave
Someone of might, and vastness.

Now to the tip-top soars my flight,
Now I fall with all my weight:
Round my head I hear unite
All the war-cries of the shade,
All the vultures of the pit,
Tempest, storm and thunderbolt,
Harsh north wind intemperate,
All the terrors that pell-mell
Beat their wings and whirl and wheel
In the deep, the void abrupt.

Pallid Night, great phantom, sparse
In unfathomable space,
High above the fearsome dome,
Looming down on every side,
Once caught Epicurus' eye.
I shall see her grim and proud
Whom Antisthenes beheld,
He who asked the wild winds 'Why?'
While her gloomy robes enfold,
Float around me in the shade.

'You are gripped by madness, mortal,'
So the cloud shall scowl. 'The Night:
Do you treat her as your portal?'
So the gloom shall growl. 'Poor poet!'
Space will tell me: 'You are lost:
Will you pass where Theban Pindar,
Hebrew David never passed?'
'It was here' shall cry the gale,
'Hesiod said "I desist!"
"No more!" said Ezekiel.'

All the shadows' devilment
Strives and fails to slow my flight,
For my back shall not be bent,
Nor my brow be fearful-white.
To the Sphinx that shrivels thought,
No less monstrous I'll appear:
For two destinies I'm wrought,
Having in the heavenly sphere
Too much human for the light,
Too much angel for the night.

2

'Copy,' the shadow tells the bard,
'Those who go in awe of God;
Cross no alien limits, nor
Bounds not lightly to be crossed:
Do not breach the dismal shore
On which darkness, dream and death
Mix in one their silent breath,
While the void, unformed and vast,
Bears away on surging flood
Vanished prophets of the past.

‘All your efforts are no use,
Wasted, all superfluous.
Take a faith: select, prefer:
No-one listens to your prayer;
The perplexity remains.
Calm infinity contains
Those who try to flee the Lord,
Those as well who rush to God,
All in one equal, infinitc,
Total stillness, total night.

‘Climb Olympus: was not Zeus
Found there by Stesichorus?
Climb Mount Horeb, still on fire
From Jehovah’s passage there.
Dreamer, those are pinnacles,
Lofty paths, and mighty goals...
From them you return despairing,
Shamed in the black shade to have
Abdicated to belief,
Angry to have been adoring!

‘The Olympian God is fume,
And the God of Sinai, night.
Nowhere does the shade relent,
Nowhere do the stars ignite.
Man should live and be content
To be man, and never tempt
Heights of ether, depths of gloom:
His flame is joined to mud and dirt.
Man is, for the sky, a spirit;
For the earth, he is a worm.

'Shakespeare, Dante, Homer! Here
Squats your smoky tripod, Art.
Art's a specious instrument:
Can it light the firmament?
Always some antique idea
Born in Elis or Chaldea
Is revived in a fresh start.
Though you glitter in your sphere,
Human spirit, don't aspire
To the Zenith with your fire.

'Socrates and Zeno first
Fed the old myths to the flame;
You to Rome's and India's gods,
Never doubting, did the same;
Like Jason's father, you immersed
In the infinitely vast,
In the nameless nowhere, someone,
A Greek or an Egyptian Ammon:
One whom old Lucretius cursed,
One whom Job, the afflicted, blessed.

'You take some chimerical
Figment of humanity,
Deck it out with aureole,
Thunder and eternity.
What you make, you then renew;
Trembling, you unveil and view
Your creation; gaze with awe,
Grant it life, beneficence,
Wisdom, bounty, providence:
Warm yourselves before this Nil.

'Dreamer, in whatever myth
He is couched, there is no Baal
That does not contain the pith
Of a glittering ideal;
Just as there is not a thorn,
No dead tree in tumbled ruin,
No impure discarded coal,
But, should just a spark ignite
In the sullen black of night,
Glows immediately bright.

See the forest undergrowth,
Sorry tilth, retained at hazard:
Rags and tatters, shivering
At the cold slither of the lizard;
Throw a coal, and this poor holly
Blossoms out majestically
Like the gold tunic of a king.
Lightning flares from shoddy briar:
All the purple tones of fire
Sleep in the woods' waste scrap of cloth.

'As a child, who throws in play
Some dry vine-twig on the flame,
Marvels at the beautiful
Coloured splendours: you're the same:
You project the blaze of all
That is dreamt of by your soul
On the first god to come your way.
Speck of dust! To your surprise
Light and fire materialise
From this monstrous Irmensul.

'With your feeble spark, derived
From a God who is perverse,
You'd establish a revived
Nature, a warmed-up universe:
Little man! You proudly preen
To have found the heart and core:
You'll destroy the nights unclean,
Love our neighbours evermore.
Worlds shall shine, I hear you crow,
On our hills, the beacons glow!

'You expect to see a dawn
Wider still and greater grown,
When your dream combusts a God
For one moment luminous.
No, dear soul, too frivolous:
Horror grips you, nothing less:
Icy temples! Dolorous
Delphi, Bethel woebegone.
Burning all the idol's wood
Hardly warms your altar-stone.'

3

I let this harsh preamble
Pass over me, I don't care,
As one lets a woodpile tremble,
Stir in the evening air.
I shall doggedly try my luck.
I've the strong will that persists,
Let the cheating riddle grumble:
Among these dubious mists,
Angry twilights, I'll be there,
Be the face that comes to look.

Life, death: the pit! Deceptive snare,
The blossoming and wilting flower,
The atom breaking from the swarm,
The nothingness that morphs its form!
No change, no afterlife, no Me,
No progress, no survival, nor
Future, nor continuity.
O yawning graves! In vain we hear
The neighing horses of the dream
Charge onward to discovery!

Does Nature deal imprisonment
To atom, germ and element,
To fail beneath unlucky stars,
Encircled by their avatars?
This whole vast world, what would it be,
If Conscience were not there to lend
Its shining light, its character?
A dark and dreadful scaling-ladder
Of rebirths with no memory,
A climb with neither goal nor end!

The grub is followed by the ghost:
O destiny! And is that all?
In life I stand at duty's post:
Have I in death no rights at all?
From rocks to angels, why is all
Tumbled, whirled senseless in the squall?
Is daybreak honest or forsworn?
Is there a life when we are born,
Before we perish? Can we prove
That the grave differs from the groove?

'I eat up men as you eat bread.'
Can it be as Tiberius said?
All the same harvest, when the Devil
Eats womankind, and Eve the apple?
Nimrod whose breath is like a storm,
Cambyses with his demon swarm,
Genghis with sword in hand, they all
Oppress, exterminate, crush, kill:
Yet they are no more criminal
Than the high mountain rocks that fall!

No! Life dark and dangerous
Moves among our troubled folk,
Sinister, mysterious,
Like a spy hidden in a cloak;
Great and small, the fools, the wise,
Perish by his messages
Tossed in blue or dreary skies:
Woe to the wicked! And the tomb
Is the brazen mouth of doom
Where God receives those calumnies.

– But it's this God that I deny,
Because, believer, empty-head,
In fashioning this world of dread
He fashioned his own calumny. –
Who says so, cool as a cadaver?
Doubt, firmly based on algebra.
From cot to coffin I must hurry,
I shake in every vertebra:
I see two sights that make me shiver:
The cradle and the ossuary.

Austere enigmas, life and death!
Reality is underneath.
Kant and Euclid and Voltaire
Hesitated, wavered there.
I'll go next, and pierce by thought
Temple and dogma, twin redoubt
Of the devout and doctrinaire,
Till my spirit finds, lays bare,
Behind Jupiter, a star,
Behind Jehovah, the azure!

For at last we have to find
The indestructible verity,
And the glorious face, behind
Those masks of obscurity;
If black bile impels the night
To snuff out the seed of life
And omnipotence and light,
In the dawn I've strong belief:
I shall make God live and move,
Burst with force of joy and love.

Can the shadows well withhold
Anything from one whose spirit
Soars with courage limitless,
Conquers time and the untold?
Greek and Jew alike the poet
Combats in the waywardness
Of their teaching and their rite,
Till he hurls himself head first,
With the world well lost, at last,
Past their obscure gods, into light!

Notes

I Guernsey

Victor Hugo lived at Hauteville House from 1856 to 1870, beyond the reach of French authority, as he was for the three preceding years in Jersey. There he wrote much of this book, and much more besides. The public can visit the house and see his own astonishing interiors. Hugo's love of wild places, especially by the sea, shines through this book and throughout his work.

ii. *Philosophers*: of the Enlightenment, Hugo's mentors: Voltaire, Rousseau, Diderot, Buffon...

iii. *George and Jean*: Georges born 1868, Jeanne 1869.

iv. Victor, sed victus: Victor, but vanquished. Hugo likes to recast Latin tags: *laetitia rerum* the joy of things, for *lacrimae*, the tears; in Section XV *laus puero*, praise to the child, for *Domino*, to the Lord.

vi. *Sirens*: lethal singing mermaids (but originally with birds' bodies), seen here as harmless. Jason, whose helmsman was Tiphys, survived because he had Orpheus to outperform them. Palinurus, helmsman of Aeneas, never heard them – he had fallen overboard, asleep, and they were passed at night in silence – but his name is the most poetic of the four.

x. *Boreas*, the north wind.

xi. *Morning – Asleep*: rapid and impressionistic, the most modern of the poems. *St Peter's*, main church of Guernsey.

xii. *An Absence*: The grandchildren's elder brother had died of meningitis, when less than a year old.

II Jean Asleep – I

Cherubino: young male charmer in Beaumarchais' play (Mozart's opera) 'The Marriage of Figaro'; the other names are from Shakespeare.

III The Moon

ii. *Avranches, Fougères*: towns in the Breton/Norman borders: Avranches is close to Mont-St-Michel. Old Yannick – he is actually called Maître Yvon – plays the Breton bagpipes, *le biniou*.

iv. *Forest of Bondy*, east of Paris.

IV Poem of the Zoo: *'Poème du Jardin des Plantes'*.

i. *Pierre-Samuel Dupont de Nemours*, politician and agronomist, held that animals talk and have souls; he moved to the USA in 1799: his son founded the huge Dupont corporation. *Buffon*, d.1788, great naturalist under Louis XV, also said *'Le style, c'est l'homme même'* – the style is the man. He ran the Jardin des Plantes. *Nisard*, Inspector of Education, a hostile critic. *Dupin*, powerful lawyer and politician, hated by Hugo.

ii. *Puss-in-Boots* and other Mother Goose tales (*Beauty and the Beast, Sleeping Beauty* etc) are from the Frenchman, Charles Perrault, 1697; La Fontaine's Fables are a little earlier. The horses of Achilles in Homer's *Iliad* 'had power of speech and reason, fleetingly'. Aesop, Phaedrus, Bidpai and Florian all wrote animal tales; Florian was a young relative of Voltaire. *Pindus*: mountain in Greece. *Ezekiel*: this is not so in Scripture, and the bald prophet was in fact Elisha.

iv. *Le Jardin des Plantes* in central Paris had been founded as a herb garden in 1626. Buffon added splendid avenues, a gallery and a laboratory. Animals arrived from 1792. In Hugo's time the lions, tigers etc were displayed in pits in the Menagerie, which is today 'the world's oldest civil zoo'. In the siege of 1870, the animals were served up as food, to Hugo among others. The main zoo is now at Vincennes. *Ounces* are lynxes, or else snow leopards. The *amphisbaena* is a mythical animal, a snake with a head at each end. It does not appear in the book of Job. Hugo likes to combine the scriptural and the classical. He has *Sépher* (one of Job's comforters, actually called Sophar in the French bible) as a rhyme for the difficult *enfer* (hell), which closes the verse. The monster and the great book of suffering lead us beyond the zoological catalogue to the idea that big cats are hellish, a verdict modified, perhaps reversed, at the end of the poem. *Colibris*: humming-birds.

v. '*Don Quixote*': a noisy entertainment – the opera came later. *Pascal* is the translator's rhyme with 'wall': Hugo rhymes '*mur*', wall, with Réaumur, on whose thermometric scale ice forms at 0°, steam at 80°. *Góngora*: exuberant Spanish poet, *fl.* 1600.

vi. *new apparitions* 'Endless forms most beautiful and most wonderful have been, and are being, evolved'. – Darwin: the concluding words of *The Origin of Species*.

vii. *Le Nôtre* designed the formal gardens of Versailles. *Boileau* wrote the rules of poetry, some of which Hugo overturned.

viii. *Nemean lion, Stymphalian birds, Erymanthian boar, Lernæan hydra*: horrid creatures killed by Hercules. *Calydon*: a wild part of Greece, where a mythical boar-hunt went terribly wrong. Fights of Hercules, flights of *Bellerophon* (on the horse Pegasus), *prophecies of Amos*: all transcendent.

x. *Leviathan*: sea-monster. *Halcyon*: mythical bird whose floating nest calms the sea; name for kingfisher.

V Old Age and Youth Together

iv. *Napoleon III*, elected President 1848, became by *coup d'état* Emperor 1852–70: after his defeat and fall Hugo returned to France. *Barbès*, a revolutionary, was saved from execution by Hugo.

vi. *The Pot of Jam*: best-known poem in the book. The dark room or cubby-hole is at Hauteville House, Guernsey.

vii. *Wicked Wolf*: from the medieval *Roman de Renard*, adapted or misremembered. *Red-Riding-Hood*: Hugo wrote *pèlerin, pèlerine*, pilgrim: the latter word can mean a hood.

x. *The sceptre's partner*: Hugo had seen a large royal coat-of-arms on the prison in Guernsey. *Jean Calas* Tried and unjustly executed for murder, rehabilitated by Voltaire. *Joan* of Arc, 'Maid of Orleans', put to death by fire 1431, beatified 1909, canonised as a saint 1920. Bishop *Dupanloup* resigned from the Academy when the atheist lexicographer Littré was elected.

VII The Immaculate Conception

In the two poems under this heading, Hugo in fact aims his rhetoric more at the concept of Original Sin. He maintains that children are entirely innocent, perhaps especially girls. *Trublet*, ridiculed by *Voltaire*; Pluche, his contemporary. *Veuillot*, a devout journalist in Hugo's time.

VIII Schoolboy Scribbles

Victor Hugo remembers his late son Charles by his inky textbook of the satirist, Juvenal. There is a character in *Les Misérables* who has learnt Latin solely in order to read Juvenal. *Nisard*, see IV.i. *Papillon* escaped from Devil's Island, long after Hugo's time (!); Bonivard was chained to a pillar 1530-36 at *Chillon*, Switzerland. (In Byron's poem: 'May none those marks efface: For they appeal from tyranny to God.') Hugo visited Chillon in 1845 for the Red Cross, and was deeply moved. Here, though, he names not Bonivard but Latude, who was mostly held in the Bastille, without trial, from 1750 to 1785.

Tantalus and a few other evildoers in Greek myth faced eternal punishment. Tantalus had water up to his chin, and fruit growing just overhead, but when he tried to eat or drink, they receded: hence 'tantalise'. Sisyphus was the stone-roller. *Nicholas Boileau* wrote the rules of poetry in *L'Art Poétique*, 1674.

IX Pepita

Back in 1811, Victor Hugo's father was a Napoleonic general in occupied Madrid. Wellington's army was about to break out of Portugal. Meanwhile we have the burlesque of young Victor's amorous awakening.

X Children, Birds and Flowers

i. *Roland*, name of heroic companion of Charlemagne. *Pau* is near Roncesvalles, scene of Roland's defining battle.

XI Stones Thrown at Jean

1871: the Paris Commune was mercilessly crushed. Belgium refused asylum to fleeing Communards. Hugo offered them shelter in his Brussels house, which was stoned by a mob, sixty strong. Jean was grazed. Hugo was expelled from Belgium.

XIII Epic Story of the Lion

i. *Irmensul*, (a pillar of) Irmino, pagan deity: Charlemagne destroyed one. *Woods worthy of a consul*, from Virgil, Eclogue IV: an epic theme in a rustic setting. *Avernus*, Italian lake, in Latin poetry an entrance to Hell.

iii. *Snowdon, Cairngorm*: actually Ossa and Pelion, mountains in Greece. The giants piled Ossa on Pelion to assault the gods on the highest peak, Olympus. The rout of the hunting army recalls Hugo's epic description of Waterloo.

XIV To Souls Flown Away

St-Leu-la-Forêt, a rural village north of Paris, summer home of the Hugo family in 1840–42. Since then Hugo had lost his pregnant daughter with her husband in a boating accident, and later his own wife, a grandchild, and his two sons.

XV Praise to the Child: Laus Puero

ii. *The Syllabus*: a Syllabus of Errors issued in 1864 by the Pope, Pius IX.

iv. *The Law of Freedom in (Higher) Education* of 1875 bore the name of Dupanloup, Bishop of Orleans, often Hugo's adversary. Hugo in 1850 had made a great speech calling for publicly funded schools to be entirely secular. In the 1880s this largely became law.

v. *Penniless Children*: Hugo gave regular beef dinners to large numbers of destitute children in Guernsey. This poem was also translated by the poet Swinburne.

vii. *Basilio*: slanderer from 'The Marriage of Figaro'.

ix. *Myrmidons*: troops of Achilles at Troy: the name might suggest Ants. *Argonne*: forest near Verdun: battles in 1792, 1871, 1918.

XVI Two Songs

Ancestor's Song: France had lost Alsace and part of Lorraine to Prussia. Hugo in 1871 opposed the peace treaty. He called for the recovery of these lands, and more, and again (as in 1849) for the United States of Europe: eternal friendship and the brotherhood of mankind.

XVIII What They Will Read Later On

i. *Austerlitz*: Napoleon's great victory in December 1805 over the Russians and Austrians, near Brno.

ii. *Cumberland*, etc: in fact Hugo refers to persons from French, not British, history, though he does name Cromwell and King Charles I.

The Furies: cruel spirits of vengeance. In the play by Aeschylus, Athena, goddess of Wisdom, gives Athens its Court of Justice, as a civilised alternative. *Inquisitor*: Hugo names Pedro de Arbuez, murdered 1485 in Zaragoza, sainted 1867. *Bossuet*, 1627–1704, great orator and exponent of doctrine. The

Edict of Nantes, 1598, brought France a period of tolerance, peace and prosperity; it was revoked by *Letellier* in 1685, many Huguenots leaving for Britain and the Netherlands.

Fraternity is a concept which English-speakers have rather left to the French. Hugo is again close to the religious view: tolerance, peace, forgiveness, grace and a mercy which proves to be simple justice.

v. *The Soul Pursuing Truth*

Epicurus, Zeno, Antisthenes: Greek philosophers of the three main schools. *Thales*, 'the first philosopher', predicted the solar eclipse of 585 BC. *Jason's father*, in myth, was boiled by Jason's vengeful wife Medea, in a pretence of rejuvenation. *Hesiod, Stesichorus, Pindar*: Greek poets.

Elis great temple of Zeus; site of Olympic Games from 776 BC. *Chaldea* where Abraham came from. *Baal, Irmensul* refer to pagan deities. *Cambyses* Persian emperor, conquered Egypt.

Brazen mouth, at Venice, in which denunciations could be placed. All are glimpsed on the poet's unflinching journey into the beyond.

Some other poems by Victor Hugo

The Expiation: Moscow, Waterloo, St Helena

From *Les Châtiments,* 1853

> *'If Hugo had written no more than the eighty lines of Waterloo, he would still be our greatest, our only epic poet.'*
> – André Bellesort

Victor Hugo came to idolise the great Napoleon, and his writings enhanced the Emperor's enduring legend. His father, a general, governed central Spain under Napoleon's brother, King Joseph. His uncle fought with distinction at Eylau. He saw Napoleon as fulfilling the Revolution. In 1848 the barricades went up in Paris, first against the monarchy, then against the new provisional government. Hugo, now a Deputy, walked with great courage between the guns to avert a massacre and restore order. France emerged with universal male suffrage. No-one argued more strongly than Hugo for Louis-Napoleon to become President; but in 1851, when the President promoted himself to Emperor, Hugo called for resistance. He was banished, spent three years in Jersey, and settled in Guernsey, returning to France only in 1870 when Napoleon III had fallen.

In Jersey he composed the three epic narratives of Moscow, Waterloo and St Helena. The recent state funerals of both Napoleon and Wellington must have intensified his emotions. (His own was to be attended by two million people, a comparable glory.) He could not accept the seizure of power, as he saw it, by both Emperors. With that perspective, he raises his historical descriptions to the moral sphere: the disasters are Napoleon's punishments. For the fourth and greatest punishment, Hugo has Napoleon wake sweating in his tomb to see his nephew's illicit regime of crooks and cronies.

For artistic effect Hugo reduces the role of Ney in the retreat from Moscow, and simplifies the battle of Waterloo, exaggerating the fate of the Guard.

(In Russia Ney commanded the rearguard, fighting every day for three months, sword in hand, repeatedly rallying his exhausted men to beat off the enemy. But at Waterloo he blundered, leading a cavalry charge without waiting for the order. The French morale broke at the sight of the Imperial Guard bringing the Emperor off the field.)

The Highest Crime

The highest crime this mortal world affords
Is to bind France, or strangle Rome with cords;
In any city, any land, to steal
From each his soul, their liberty from all.
To press into the court august, to draw
Sword in the temple, and strike dead the law:
A people fettered: from a crime so base
God of the tranquil dream turns not his face.
The deed once done, no mercy! From azure
Fastnesses, Retribution, slow but sure,
Moves on her course. She comes, her visage calm,
Her lash of brazen spikes beneath her arm.

Moscow

Snow fell. By his own conquest overpowered,
For the first time the eagle's head was lowered.
In slow retreat the emperor (dark days!)
Left in his wake charred Moscow still ablaze.
Snow fell. Harsh winter loosed her avalanche,
And white expanse led on to white expanse.
Rank went unrecognised, the colours blurred,
The once Grand Army had become a herd.
The flanks and centre could not be descried.
Snow fell. The wounded huddled up inside
Dead horses' bellies; buglers, white with frost,
Stiff in the saddle, frozen at their post,
Manned windswept bivouacs, erect, alone,
The brass clamped silent to their lips of stone.
Shells, bullets, grapeshot rained, with every flake.
Guardsmen, surprised to learn their limbs could shake,
Trudged, pensive; ice on grey moustaches bristled.
Snow fell unceasingly; the cold wind whistled;
Onward across uncharted wastes they trod,

Starving and barefoot on the frozen mud,
No longer living hearts, nor soldiery,
A dream that strayed in fog, a mystery,
A string of shadows on funereal sky.
The fearsome wasteland stretched out endlessly,
A mute avenging presence all around.
The sky and thick-massed snow without a sound
Made a great shroud round the great army lying;
Each was alone; each knew that he was dying.
Could they escape this vast and sombre power?
Two foes! the Czar, the north: the north, more dour.
Who lay down, died. Confused, dejected, solemn,
They fled: the barren waste devoured the column.
Gun-carriages were burned, the guns were ditched.
The snow all puckered over drapes rough-pitched
Marked where his regiments in slumber lay.
Hannibal routed! Attila's reckoning-day!
Barrows, kegs, stretchers, fugitives, wounded, slain,
Crammed bridges till they trod dry ground again.
Ten thousand slept, a hundred woke next day.
Late leader of an army, Marshal Ney
Traded his pocket-watch with three Cossacks.
Each night brought skirmishes, alerts, attacks!
Each night these phantoms grasped their guns; they heard
Yelps of the bald marauding carrion-bird:
Saw hurtling at them monstrous looming forms,
Horrible squadrons, men in bestial swarms.
Thus a whole army perished in the night.
The emperor stood at hand, took in the sight;
He was a tree to which the axe was laid:
Upon this giant there climbed with deadly blade
Misfortune, the grim woodman; long intact
And proud the tree had stood; now, rudely hacked,
The living oak shook at the vengeful blast
Of doom, and saw his branches fall at last.
All ranks were dying. Remnants round his tent,
Loving him as his shadow came and went

Across the canvas, trusting in his star,
Charged fate with treason! Now the emperor,
Suddenly, deeply stricken by the rout,
His spirit overcome and full of doubt,
Turned towards God: the man of glory quailed:
Such was his due for having somehow failed:
His expiation. This he seemed to know;
Before his legions scattered on the snow,
Thus said Napoleon, pale and wondering:
'O Lord of hosts, is this the chastening?'
He listened; and his name was called, and lo,
One in the shadow spoke, who told him: No!

Waterloo

Waterloo! Waterloo! disastrous field!
Like a wave swelling in an urn brim-filled,
Your ring of hillsides, valleys, woods and heath
Saw grim battalions snarled in pallid death.
On this side France, against her Europe stood:
God failed the heroes in the clash of blood!
Destiny faltered, victory turned tail.
O Waterloo, alas! I weep, I fail!
Those last great soldiers of the last great war
Were giants, each the whole world's conqueror:
Crossed Alps and Rhine, made twenty tyrants fall.
Their soul sang in the brazen bugle-call!

Night fell; the fight was burning fierce, and black.
He grasped the victory, was on the attack,
Held Wellington pinned down against a wood.
Eyeglass in hand, observing all, he stood:
Now the dark midpoint of the battle's fires,
A throbbing clutch of frightful, living briars;

Now the horizon, sombre as the sea.
He gave a sudden, joyous cry: 'Grouchy!'
'Twas Blücher! Hope changed sides, the combat swayed,
Like wildfire surged the howling fusillade.
The guns of England broke the squares of France.
Amid the cries of slaughtered combatants,
The plain where our torn banners shook and spread
Was but a fiery chasm, furnace-red.
Regiments tumbled down like lengths of wall.
Like stalks of corn the great drum-majors fall,
Their plumes, full-length, enormous on the ground;
And every view revealed a hideous wound.
Grim carnage! fatal moment! There he stands,
Anxious, the battle pliant in his hands.
Behind a little hill was massed the Guard,
The last great hope, supreme and final word!
'Send in the Guard!' he cries, and grenadiers
In their white gaiters, lancers, cuirassiers,
Dragoons that Rome would count among her sons,
Men who unleashed the thunder of the guns,
The men of Friedland and of Rivoli,
Black busbies, gleaming helms, in panoply,
Knowing this solemn feast must be their last,
Salute their god, erect amid the blast.
'Long live the emperor!' A single cry;
Then at slow march, bands playing, steadily,
The Guard came smiling on, the Imperial,
Where English salvoes raked the crucible.
Alas! Napoleon with gaze intense
Watched the advance: he saw his regiments
Under the sulphurous venom of the guns:
He saw those troops of stone and steel at once
Melted, all melted in the pit of death,
As melts the wax beneath the brazier's breath.
Steadfast and stoic, sloped arms and unbowed head,
They went. None flinched. Then sleep, heroic dead! ...
All the remainder stood and stared, held hard,

Motionless watched the death-throes of the Guard.
All of a sudden now they see her rise:
Defeat! Grim-faced, with loud despairing cries,
Putting the proudest regiments in dread,
Turning their banners to a tattered shred,
At certain times, a wraith, a smoke-wreathed ghost,
Rears up erect and huge amid the host.
Wringing her hands, to soldiers terrified,
Defeat appeared: 'Run for your lives!' she cried.
Run for your lives! shame, dread! each soldier bawled:
Across the fields, distraught, wild-eyed, appalled,
Between the dusty wagons and the kegs
As if a wind came blowing on their legs,
In ditches rolled, in cornfields crouched to hide,
Their shakos, coats, guns, eagles cast aside
Under the Prussian swords, each veteran
(O sorrow!) howled with terror, wept and ran.
At once, like burning straw by tempests blown,
All the Grand Army's battle-roar was gone.
Here we may stand, and dream: for from this site
They fled, who put the universe to flight.
Forty years on, this shunned and dismal field,
This Waterloo, this crevice of the world,
Where God piled nullity on nullity,
Still trembles to have seen the giants flee!

Napoleon saw them pouring like a flood:
Men, steeds, drums, flags. Facing his fate he stood,
Confused, as if repining; then he said,
Raising his hands to heaven: 'My soldiers dead,
I and my empire broken in the dust.
Is this thy chastening, O God most just?'
Amid the cries, the guns, the tumult, lo!
He heard the voice that gave him answer: No!

St Helena

He fell; and God changed Europe's iron bands.

Far in the fog-bound seas a vile rock stands,
Belched up by old volcanoes. Destiny
Took nails and clamps and neck-irons, gleefully,
Seized him who stole the thunder, living, pale,
And dragged him to the grizzled peak, to nail
Him down, and with a mocking laugh to start
The vulture England gnawing at his heart.

Immeasurable splendour, passed away!
From earliest sunrise till the end of day
Ever alone, abandoned, caged in prison;
A redcoat near; beyond, the sea's horizon.
Bare rocks, grim woods, depression, emptiness:
Sails passing, fleeing into hopelessness.
The sound of winds and waves for evermore!
Farewell, white horse that Caesar spurs to war,
Farewell the pounding drums, the stratagem,
The purple tent, the plumes, the diadem!
No quaking prostrate kings inferior;
No robe trailed over them; no emperor.
Napoleon was reduced to Bonaparte.
He thought of Moscow burning, sick at heart
As Roman bleeding from the Parthian bolt:
An English corporal, to bid him Halt!
Kings held his son; his wife was spoken for;
Worse than a pig that wallows in a sewer,
His senate cursed him, worshipping no more.
When ocean winds fall still, he walked the shore
On cliffs that crumbled in black heaps of stone,
The dark waves' captive, dreaming and alone.

As bygone battles still amazed his eye,
With rueful pride on hill and sea and sky
He cast his thoughts, to stray on high adventure.
Grandeur and glory, void! the calm of nature!
Eagles pass by, not knowing who he is.
The kings, his jailers, took their compasses
And closed him in a ring inflexible.
He sickened. Death more and more visible
Rose in the night and grew before his eyes,
Like the cold breaking of a strange sunrise.
His soul, that fluttered still, was almost fled.
At last he laid his sword upon his bed,
And took his place, and said 'This is the day.'
Wrapped in his old Marengo cloak he lay.
Nile, Danube, Tiber: battles on his brow
Gathered. Said he: 'I am unfettered now!
I am victorious! Come, my eagles, fly!'
And as he turned his head aside to die,
Intruding in the empty house he saw
Hudson Lowe watching through the half-closed door.
The kings beneath their heel had trampled him!
'Full measure!' cried the giant; 'to the brim!
Now it is finished! God whom I implore,
Thy chastening's done!' The voice said, 'There is More!'

June 1871

[The End of the Paris Commune]

A woman told me this: 'I took to flight.
My baby at my breast, poor little mite,
Cried, and I was afraid she might be heard.
Imagine, Sir, the child was two months old,
No stronger than a fly. I tried and tried
To stop her mouth with kisses: but she cried,
Rattling. She would have fed, but I was dry:
I only wept. That's how a night went by.
I hid behind a door. I saw the glint
Of arms, the guns of killers, on the hunt
For my husband. Morning broke. Behind that door,
A curse on it! my darling cried no more.
Sir, she was dead: I touched her, she was cold.
I ran, not caring if I too was killed,
Anywhere, with my daughter. People called
Out to me, but I fled, I don't know where,
Into the fields, and dug a hole with bare
Hands, in some paddock, in a place of shade.
It's hard to bury one your breast has fed!
I laid to rest in earth my angel, sleeping.'

The father stood beside her: he was weeping.

from *The Terrible Year*

Good Advice to Lovers

An ogre in the woods of Muscovy
Adored a fairy fay. So keen was he,
So desperate the brute to wed this lady,
His mounting passion almost drove him crazy.
The ogre combed his hide one winter's day,
Went calling at the palace of the fay,
And told the usher he was Prince Ogrousky.
The fairy had a son, we don't know whose. She
Was out that day. The child, a fair, plump lad,
Nourished on cakes and cream, whom someone had
Fathered, Odysseus-like, on this Calypso,
Was in the porch, and playing with his hoop. So
They were left sitting in the antechamber.
What does one do when snow falls in December,
Having no prospect of a conversation?
The ogre opted for a degustation.
It is a trifle fast, and not too bright,
Even for an ogre and a Muscovite,
To gobble up your neighbour's little mite.
An ogre's yawn can match his appetite.
When she returned, no child. The staff advised;
She saw the ogre's mouth was oversized;
'Have you seen my pretty child at all?' she cried;
'I've eaten it,' the simple hulk replied.

A blunder. If you hope to please, for sure
Don't eat the child whose mother you adore.

from *Toute la Lyre, 1873*

Boaz Asleep

from *The Legend of the Ages*

Hugo's gigantic project *La Légende des Siècles* purports to cover the whole span of the human story, drawing on scripture, classical antiquity, medieval history and the downright legendary. It is a vast unfinished series of separate poems, portraying individuals and episodes in epic, moral or satirical vein. Baudelaire called the whole collection 'the only modern epic possible'.

The scriptural story of Boaz is found in the Book of Ruth. Hugo embellishes it with elements borrowed from the stories of Abraham and Jesse, and much else besides. Proust called it the most beautiful poem of the century.

This translation of *Booz Endormi* is written without using the letter e, a constraint found in Georges Perec's novel *La Disparition*, and Gilbert Adair's translation, *A Void*.

As Boaz Was Dozing

Boaz had cut his corn and sought his cot.
A hard day's winnowing had fairly worn
Him out, and laid him in his usual spot.
His bins stood not far off, chock-full of corn.

Boaz was old, and rich in corn and grain,
Nor loth, for all his gold, to act aright:
His mill ran limpid, with no muddy stain;
His smithy cast no dark satanic light.

His hoary locks hung smooth as April rill.
His tilth had no tight fist, no hint of gall:
Should a poor woman pass, it was his will
That handy stalks of corn should thickly fall.

Boaz trod upright, far from shady ways,
In candid purity and snowy gown,
And always, as a public fountain plays,
Flung many a grainsack charitably down:

A loyal kinsman and a pious lord,
Unstinting, though not prodigal of hand;
As no young man, by womankind ador'd:
Youth has good looks, a patriarch is grand!

Old folk, backtracking to our primal spring,
Quit dubious days for dawning glory bright.
A young man's iris is a blazing thing;
An old man's, if you look, is full of light.

So Boaz lay that night among his own,
Dark knots of farmhands, with his stooks on show,
As big as dust-hills, if you hadn't known.
This was particularly long ago.

No kings wrought Judah's laws, but Dayanim;
Man was nomadic, and still gaping stood
At giants' footprints that astonish'd him,
On soil still damp and soft from Noah's flood.

Jacob lay still, and Judith; Boaz too
Blind and oblivious in his arbour lay.
Now from on high, a yawning portal through,
To him a holy vision found its way.

It was a vision of a vast oak, going
Up from his loins towards a cobalt sky,
And, link by link, a clan, a nation growing:
A king who sang; a dying god, hung high.

Said Boaz, in his spirit murmuring,
'Forty on forty birthdays, Lord! I pil'd;
How shall all this from my old body spring?
I cannot boast a consort, nor a child.

'Thou know'st that long ago my faithful fair,
Lord God Almighty, quit my couch for yours.
Twin souls conjoint, a still-commingling pair,
Gliding in convoy through oblivion's doors.

'That I should found a family? How so?
How should my loins now bring a brood to birth?
For in our youth triumphant mornings glow,
And, out of night, day springs victorious forth;

But I am shaky as a birch in snow,
A widow-man, on whom long shadows sink.
Towards my tomb my soul is winging low,
Just as a thirsty ox bows down to drink.'

All this in mystic vision Boaz said,
Turning to God his drowsy orbs, all calm;
Nor thought a woman at his foot was laid.
So daisy blows, unmark'd by lofty palm.

Boaz was all unconscious in his cot;
At his foot, humbly, Ruth from Moab lay,
Half-clad, awaiting dawn, and who knows what
Illumination, born of waking day.

Boaz wist not that Ruth was lying by;
Ruth had no inkling what was in God's mind...
Floral aromas, dill and dittany;
Fragrant with amaranth, Galgala's wind.

O nuptial pomp! How grand a shadow cast!
No doubt a holy choir was gambolling,
all shyly; for an unknown form slid past,
Cobalt in colour: possibly, a wing.

From Boaz' lungs and throat a rhythmic wind
Struck chords with murmurs born of mossy rills.
It was a month that's naturally kind,
With lily-blossoms glorious on hills.

Ruth musing, Boaz snoozing; darkling sward;
Far off, a woolly flock was dully clinking,
As from on high abundant bounty pour'd;
A happy hour, that brings out lions, drinking.

In Ur and Ziph and Mizpah, not a sound.
A thin, bright moon was shining on its way
Among night's blooms, down a dark sky, profound,
Inlaid with starry studs; and so Ruth lay,

Half-glancing through a shawl, and calm at last...
Bringing a bounty in that grows not old,
What god, what swain, thought Ruth, has idly cast
On starry corn his falchion wrought of gold?

Victor Hugo's Life

1802 Born at Besançon. Father a military officer.
1804 Napoleon becomes Emperor.
1806 In Italy. Father, now a Major, captures Fra Diavolo.
1807 Uncle's bravery at Napoleonic battle of Eylau.
1811 In Madrid. Father, a General, governs central Spain.
1815 Waterloo. Napoleon falls. Bourbon king returns.
1818 Victor's parents separate.
1819 Guest of Chateaubriand: resolves to surpass him.
1820 Royal pension for his poems. *Bug-Jargal*, Haiti novel.
1821 Mother dies, staunchly Catholic and conservative.
1822 Victor marries Adèle Foucher. Brother insane.
1823 Iceland novel, *Han d'Islande*. Baby son Léopold dies.
1824 *Nouvelles Odes*. Daughter Léopoldine born.
1825 Légion d'Honneur. Attends coronation of Charles X.
1826 *Odes et Ballades*. Son Charles born.
1827 Ode to [Napoleon's] column in La Place Vendôme. Stage play with important preface, *Cromwell*.
1828 Father dies. Son François-Victor born.
1829 Poems, *Les Orientales*.
1830 Stage play, *Hernani*, in verse: metre too free for some patrons: fighting in the stalls. Novel, *Le Dernier Jour d'un condamné* (*Last Day of a Condemned Man*): passionate foe of death penalty.
Daughter Adèle born. A second Revolution: barricades and gunfire: king replaced by cousin, Louis-Philippe.
'Liberty Leading the People' painted by Delacroix.
1831 Novel, *Notre-Dame de Paris* (aka *The Hunchback...*).
Poems, *Les Feuilles d'automne (Autumn Leaves)*.
1832 Barricades (as seen in *Les Misérables*): bullets fly: Hugo in crossfire.
1832–48 Living at 6, Place des Vosges, today a museum.
1832 Play: *Le Roi s'amuse* (Verdi's opera *Rigoletto*): banned.
1833 Plays: *Lucrèce Borgia, Marie Tudor*. Lifelong lover of actress Juliette Drouet, who appears in both plays.
1833–39 Travel in Brittany, Normandy, Belgium, Alsace, Switzerland, Provence. Poems, *Les Chants du Crépuscule (Songs of Twilight)*; essays; two plays.
1841 Elected to Académie Française, after three rebuffs.
1843 Léopoldine marries Charles Vacquerie. Hugo in Spain: while returning, he reads news of their death with unborn first child, in a boating accident at Villequier. He abandons literature for politics.
1845 Raised to peerage of France. Lover of Mme Biard, pursued by husband. Jailed; released as a peer. King squares Biard. Beginnings of novel *Les Misérables*.

1848 (February) Barricades, revolution. Republic. Senior poet Lamartine heads provisional government. All adult males can vote. (June) Elected to Assembly.
Barricades again. Hugo is among sixty deputies sent to restore order. Reckless courage; armed suppression.
Supports Napoleon's nephew, Prince Louis-Napoleon, who is elected France's first President. Many speeches in the progressive cause.

1849 Elected president of World Peace Congress, in Paris. Great speech for Liberty. Both sons, journalists, jailed.

1851 Louis-Napoleon's *coup d'état*. Hugo is incensed: he resists and has to flee. False passport and disguise arranged by Juliette: goes to Belgium. Banished from France.

1852 Napoleon III crowned by Archbishop of Paris. Hugo's prose work, *Napoléon-le-Petit*. He arrives in Jersey, with family. *Châtiments*: wounding poems.

1854 Spiritualism. Work on *Contemplations*: poems.

1855 Queen Victoria visits Paris: angry words of others in sons' Jersey newspaper. Hugo expelled from Jersey. Thanks to Juliette, he is able to settle in Guernsey.

1856 With proceeds of books published in Brussels, he buys Hauteville House, Guernsey. Adorns it profusely with carved wood and ceramics. Prolific years of writing:-

1856–9 Work on poems: *La Légende des Siècles (The Legend of the Ages), Chansons des Rues et des Bois (Songs of the Woods and Ways);* novels: *Les Travailleurs de la Mer (Toilers of the Sea), Les Misérables.*

1859 Success of *La Légende*. Refuses the emperor's general amnesty. 'I shall share to the end the exile of Liberty. When Liberty returns, I shall return.'

1864 *William Shakespeare*: glorifies many writers of genius.

1865 Poems, *Les Chansons des Rues et des Bois.*

1866 Novel, *Les Travailleurs de la Mer*. All these books acclaimed.

1868 Birth of grandson Georges, son of Charles. Wife dies.

1869 Birth of Georges' sister Jeanne.

1870 Both children in Guernsey. France defeated by Prussia.
Emperor falls. Paris besieged. Hugo returns to a tumultuous welcome. Scathing words to the Prussians

1871 and to the Assembly, which he quits. Son Charles dies: great crowds at funeral. Commune in Paris mercilessly crushed. Hugo offers sanctuary to fugitives.
Hugo, grandchildren and four women in Brussels house stoned by mob. Jeanne grazed by stone. Hugo expelled from Belgium.

1872 Daughter Adèle elopes, is deserted, confined in asylum.

1873	In Guernsey, without family: novel, *Quatrevingt-treize* ('93). In Paris with family: son François-Victor dies.
1876	Elected to Senate.
1877	Three very successful books. Poems: *La Légende des Siècles (Legend of the Ages)*: epic work continued. *L'Art d'être Grand-Père (How to be a Grandfather)*. Possible monarchist coup prompts *Histoire d'un Crime*.
1878	Heart attack. Goes to Guernsey. Will love only Juliette.
1881	Eightieth year: in Paris: enormous public celebrations.
1883	Juliette Drouet dies.
1885	Victor Hugo dies. State funeral, two million people in the streets.

Hugo's Poems in English Translation

The Distance, The Shadows: Harry Guest, Anvil Poetry Press, 1981, 2002
Selected Poems of Victor Hugo: E.H. & A.M. Blackmore, Chicago U.P., 2001, 2004
Victor Hugo, Selected Poetry: Brooks Haxton, Penguin, 2002.
Victor Hugo, Selected Poetry: Steven Monte, Carcanet, 2001.
All these books have both French and English text.

Biographies of Hugo

Victor Hugo: Graham Robb, Picador, 1998.
Victor Hugo: Samuel Edwards, New English Library, 1971.
Victor Hugo: A Realistic Biography of the Great Romantic: M. Josephson, Doubleday Doran 1942 and Jorge Pinto Books, 2006.
Olympio: The Life of Victor Hugo: André Maurois, 1956, 1985
Victor Hugo: Joanna Richardson, 1976

CDs of Hugo's Poems Set to Music

Mélodies sur des Poèmes de Victor Hugo: Felicity Lott soprano, Graham Johnson piano: Harmonia Mundi 1999
Victor Hugo en Musique: Konstantin Wolff bass-baritone, Trung Sam *piano*: Harmonia Mundi 1999
Victor Hugo – Poèmes en Musique: Marie Devellereau *soprano*, Philippe Cassard *piano*: Ambroisie 2008
Mélodies sur des Poèmes de Victor Hugo: Cécile Eloir *mezzo-contralto*, Cyprien Katsaris *piano*: Saphir, 2004
Serge Kerval chante Victor Hugo: Arion, 2009

Victor Hugo as seen by other Poets

Charles Baudelaire

"When you think of what French poetry was
before he appeared, and what a rejuvenation
it has undergone since his arrival...
it is impossible not to consider him
one of thosc ***rare and providential minds***
who in the domain of literature
bring about ***the salvation of us all.***"

Elizabeth Barrett Browning

An excerpt from her plea to Napoleon III, which was never sent

"...It is, indeed, precisely because he cannot be excused that, I think, he might worthily be forgiven. For this man, whatever else he is not, is a great poet of France, and the Emperor, who is the guardian of her other glories, should remember him and not leave him out. Ah, sire, what was written on 'Napoleon le Petit' does not touch your Majesty; but what touches you is, that no historian of the age should have to write hereafter, 'While Napoleon III reigned, Victor Hugo lived in exile.'...Ah, sire, you are great enough! You can allow for the peculiarity of the poetical temperament, for the temptations of high gifts ... Forgive this enemy, this accuser, this traducer. Disprove him by your generosity. Let no tear of an admirer of his poetry drop upon your purple. Make an exception of him, as God made an exception of him when He gave him genius, and call him back – without condition – to his country and his daughter's grave."

A.C. Swinburne: from his long poem 'To Victor Hugo'

Praised above men be thou,
Whose laurel-laden brow,
Made for the morning, droops not in the night;
Praised and beloved, that none
Of all thy great things done
Flies higher than thy most equal spirit's flight;
Praised, that nor doubt nor hope could bend
Earth's loftiest head, found upright to the end.

Alfred Tennyson: Sonnet 'To Victor Hugo'

Victor in Drama*, Victor in Romance,
Cloud-weaver of phantasmal hopes and fears,
French of the French, and Lord of human tears;
Child-lover; Bard whose fame-lit laurels glance
Darkening the wreaths of all that would advance,
Beyond our strait, their claim to be thy peers;
Weird Titan by thy winter weight of years
As yet unbroken, Stormy voice of France!
Who dost not love our England—so they say;
I know not—England, France, all man to be
Will make one people ere man's race be run:
And I, desiring that diviner day,
Yield thee full thanks for thy full courtesy
To younger England in the boy my son.

'Drama' in 1880. 'Poesy' originally in 1877.

Gérard de Nerval: 'Notre-Dame of Paris'

Notre-Dame's old. Who knows if, by and by,
She, who saw Paris born, shall see her die?
Ages shall pass. Time, as the wolf subdues
The ox, shall bring her heavy carcass down
With his dull tooth, shall twist her iron thews,
And gnaw her skeleton of ancient stone.

From every land on earth a throng shall stream
To view the dismal ruin, and shall dream,
Reading the fable that great Victor made:
They'll see a vision of the hallowed pile,
Mighty and splendid in its antique style,
Rise up before them like a spectral shade!

Jean Cassou: from '33 Sonnets of the Resistance'

Since cherry-time I've nursed, deep down,
a wound that opens every day,
while by the walls of Anytown
lilacs and suns and breezes play.

Land of blue roofs and grey refrains
that bleeds in love's romantic dress,
tell me why each old yard enchains
my life with tears and rustiness.

I teach the pixies on my way
about Fantine, about Cosette.
The playground tree shall soon repeat

a rousing tale: one day, one day ...
Stream forth, bright dawn, stream forth in spate,
when fists have guns to spark the fray!

Robert Desnos: 'The Legacy'

Hugo! So here's your name on every wall!
Deep in the Pantheon, turn in your grave,
And ask: who's done this? Hitler! Goebbels! They've
Done it, the guttersnipes: Pétain, Laval,

Bonnard, Brinon: accomplished traitors all,
High on the hog. They've done it, and they must
Face retribution, merciless and just;
And there are not that many names at all.

These mindless and uncultured men have made
A smokescreen for their filthy escapade:
'The fellow's dead and gone,' apparently.

The fellow's dead. Yet his bequest is clear:
His legacy is signed and proven here,
Witnessed by France; we call it Liberty.

Gérard de Nerval (1808–55), sublime poet of the Chimeras, admired Hugo's poetry, and his own was admired in return. He wrote this in response to Hugo's novel of 1831.

Jean Cassou (1897–1986) composed his *33 Sonnets* in his head in 1941–2, while imprisoned by the Vichy government without writing materials. Cherry-time refers to 'Au Temps des Cerises', a song of 1871; Cosette is the waif in Hugo's *Les Misérables*, Fantine is her mother. Later, Cassou created France's National Museum of Modern Art.

Robert Desnos (1900–45), a Surrealist and like Cassou a resistant, wrote this poem in 1943 when posters in occupied Paris claimed Hugo as a supporter of the regime. Desnos went on to write three great poetic sequences against the Occupation, and dozens of poems for children, before he was deported, to die at Terezin.

The Translator

Timothy Adès is a British translator-poet who likes to work with rhyme and metre. He has awards for translating Victor Hugo, Jean Cassou, Alfonso Reyes and Robert Desnos, and has translated Bertolt Brecht, Ángelos Sikelianós, Ricarda Huch, Gérard de Nerval and Louise Labé. Many of his versions are on the Brindin website. He made all the translations in this volume.

Other Poetry Translations by Timothy Adès

Alfonso Reyes: *Homer in Cuernavaca* (TLS Valle-Inclán Prize)
Translation & Literature, Edinburgh, 2001

Jean Cassou: *33 Sonnets of the Resistance and other poems*
Arc Publications, 2002

Robert Desnos: *Sirène-Anémone and other poems*
Translation & Literature, Edinburgh, 2005

Bertolt Brecht: *Selected Rhymed Poems*
Translation & Literature, Edinburgh, 2006

Jean Cassou: *The Madness of Amadis and other poems*
Agenda Editions, 2008

Robert Desnos: *Six Poems*
PN Review, 2011

> *Desnos* 'The translations are startlingly good.' – *Michael Schmidt*
>
> *Cassou* 'Triumphant… it is difficult to see how a free-verse translation could have achieved a comparable result.' – *Peter France*
>
> 'An arduous task performed admirably well' – *John Pilling*
>
> 'We are fortunate … creatively vigorous … personal dedication …' – *Will Stone*
>
> 'Adès has the enviable gift of lyrical lucidity. He captures the true heart of each poem … That is why so scrupulous, so inventive, so professional, so poetic a translation as this one is so welcome.' – *Harry Guest*

Other Books of Translated Poetry from Hearing Eye

Jacques Prévert: Selected Poems
Sarah Lawson

The Poems of Sulpicia
John Heath-Stubbs

Poet for Poet (Akhmatova, Pasternak, Aranzon and other Russian poets; Hikmet, Rifat, and six more from the Turkish)
Richard McKane

Collected Poems and Selected Translations
A.C. Jacobs
(Co-published with The Menard Press)

Home Bloody Home/Dome Prokleti Dome
Miroslav Jančić

Between Languages/Zwischen Sprachen
Ingeborg Santor, John Rety, Ruth Ingram

Mountain Language/Lingua di Montagna
Stephen Watts & Cristina Viti

Journey Across Breath/Tragitto nel respiro
Stephen Watts & Cristina Viti

Panther and Gazelle, Poems from Paula Ludwig's *Dem Dunklen Gott*
Selected and translated by Martina Thomson